Teaching Number Sense

# Teaching Number Sense

Julia Anghileri

continuum

Continuum International Publishing Group
The Tower Building                 80 Maiden Lane
11 York Road                       Suite 704
London                             New York
SE1 7NX                            NY 10038

**British Library Cataloguing-in-Publication Data**
A catalogue record for this book is available from the British Library.

ISBN: 978-0-8264-8686-8 (hardback); 978-0-8264-8687-5 (paperback)

Library of Congress Cataloguing-in-Publication Data
A catalog record for this book is available from the Library of Congress.

Typeset by YHT Ltd, London
Printed and bound in Great Britain by Biddles Ltd., King's Lynn, Norfolk

# Contents

For Ellie, Evie, Emmeline, Flora and Mia – the next generation of mathematical thinkers!

# List of Figures

List of Figures

# Making Sense of Numbers

Every teacher can sympathize with the frustration felt by a child who cannot solve apparently straightforward and simple arithmetic problems. As soon as symbols are introduced there are children who become confused and unsure, often despite considerable effort on their own and their teacher's part. When older children struggle to solve ? − 4 = 9 or 100 ÷ 25 = ? instead of *recognizing* the number relations involved, it is probable that they are seeking to identify an appropriate *procedure* to solve the problem whilst other children are able to use facts they already know. It is not only effort that gives some children a facility with numbers, but an awareness of relationships that enable them to interpret new problems in terms of results they remember. Children who have this awareness and the ability to work flexibly to solve number problems are said to have a 'feel' for numbers or 'number sense'. What characterizes children with 'number sense' is their ability to make generalizations about the patterns and processes they have met and to link new information to their existing knowledge. How to teach the connections involved in developing number sense will be the central focus of this book which will highlight the key ideas at each stage in children's learning.

## Number sense and the school curriculum

In the past, 'arithmetic' has meant multiplication tables and the four rules of number (that is, the correct formal methods of performing written addition, subtraction, multiplication and division), and the meaning of 'arithmetic' has over time become limited to performance in standard algorithms without an underlying understanding. In society today, there is general acceptance that 'drill and practice' of taught routines will not prepare children for life in a technological society and that teaching approaches need to focus on the links that demonstrate the logical structure underlying numbers and number operations. Rather than being shown how to do written calculations, children are to be encouraged to work mentally, to observe patterns, to predict results and to talk about the connections that can be made.

Reform of the mathematics curriculum has led to a shift from teaching standard procedures for calculating, to enabling children to observe patterns and relationships, and make connections so that they develop insight and a 'feel' for numbers (Anghileri, 2001a). The Cockcroft report used the phrase 'at-homeness with numbers' to describe one of the desirable attributes of a 'numerate adult' (Cockcroft, 1982). More recently, the UK *National Numeracy Strategy Framework for Teaching Mathematics from Reception to Year 6* uses the term 'numeracy' to identify 'the proficiency in number that involves a confidence and competence with numbers' requiring 'an understanding of the number system, a repertoire of computational skills and an inclination and ability to solve number problems in a variety of contexts' (DfEE, 1999, p. 4). 'Numeracy' goes beyond the requirement of teaching written calculating procedures to involve both mental calculation and estimation as efficient processes for calculating. There are increased roles for oral work, for 'choosing' appropriate strategies, for using calculators and for reflecting on and explaining both the processes and the results of any calculation.

Curriculum reforms are widespread throughout the world and typified by the United States' *Principles and Standards for School Mathematics* (National Council for Teachers of Mathematics, 2000), and Australia's *National Statement on Mathematics for Australian Schools* (Australian Education Council, 1991) where the identification of 'number sense' is a major essential outcome of the school curriculum. This 'number sense' which is widely used in reform documents refers to 'flexibility' and 'inventiveness' in strategies for calculating and is a reaction to overemphasis on computational procedures devoid of thinking. It refers not only to the development of understanding but also to the nurturing of a positive attitude and confidence that have been lacking in more dated curricula.

## The beginnings of number sense

By watching, listening and copying, children will initially learn isolated facts, but from the earliest stages they can be encouraged to see different ways that numbers are used and the connections that underlie their use. The number 6, for example, will not only be known as the name associated with a set of six objects, but also as the number after 5 and before 7 (as in children's ages), and 6 may also be recognized as a pattern of '2 and 2 and 2' (as seen on a dice) or '4 and 2' (counting wheels on a car and a bike) or 'double 3' (as another way to see the pattern on a dice). As their experiences of individual numbers progress, children can quickly become aware of how each number can be related to many others.

Early experiences with number operations will also provide important links across many structures that underpin children's understanding. Adding one more to a collection, for example, does not mean that the whole collection needs to be re-counted as the next number word in the counting sequence gives the new total. Similarly, taking one away gives the previous counting number. In this way, connections are established between addition, subtraction and counting with links that will form the foundations for effective calculating strategies that will be discussed in later chapters.

Number sense is highly personalized and relates not only to those ideas about number that have been established but also to *how* these have been established. It involves a way of thinking that enables children to identify quickly important relationships, such as recognizing that '32 ÷ 16' will prove significantly less problematic than '32 ÷ 17', or that '47 − 38' is effectively calculated by 'adding on to 38'. It also involves the ability to work flexibly with numbers and operations, for example knowing not only that '48' is '40 + 8', but also that it is '50 − 2' and 'double 24', and that '8 × 1/4' is not only '8 lots of 1/4' but also '8 ÷ 4'. The way numbers relate to each other, the possibilities for different representations and the meanings that can be associated with different operations will all play a key role in establishing the connections that are crucial in developing number sense.

## The goals in teaching number sense

The skills and understanding needed in preparation for living in the 21st century are different from those expected of previous generations (Brown, 2001). There is now an expectation that individuals will use their initiative in making connections between real-life problems and appropriate mathematical representations, and that they will respond flexibly in finding appropriate ways to tackle them.

> Number sense ... reflects an inclination and an ability to use numbers and quantitative methods as a means of communicating, processing and interpreting information. It results in an expectation that mathematics has a certain regularity.
>
> (McIntosh *et al.*, 1992)

Today assessment tasks have also been developed to match the changing requirements. They are no longer stereotypical numerical calculations that require standard written procedures for calculating but assessments include complex problem-solving, often in 'real-life' settings. By the end of primary school children are also expected to be competent users of calculators, and national assessment tasks are designed to assess this competence.

The final report of the Numeracy Taskforce expects that 'numerate pupils ... should:

- have a sense of the size of a number and where it fits into the number system;
- know by heart number facts such as number bonds, multiplication tables, division fact, doubles and halves;
- use what they know by heart to figure out answers mentally;
- calculate accurately and efficiently, both mentally and on paper, drawing on a range of calculation strategies...'

(DfEE, 1998, p. 11)

Children are expected to extract information from charts and tables, to calculate with missing digits and to investigate number patterns where asking appropriate questions will help to identify numerical relationships. They are expected to make choices about the most appropriate procedures, including the decision whether or not to use a calculator. These ideas mark a new departure for mathematics so that isolated procedures for calculating are not adequate, and teaching children to make connections has become a crucial requirement.

## How is number sense developed?

From the earliest stages of learning about numbers, children can be making connections that will establish flexibility in their thinking that is characteristic in developing number sense. Some links between numbers are established through patterns in counting and the following chapters will show how teaching children about counting is an important preparation for calculating. Counting here does not mean only the 'unitary' counting in ones that is a child's first experience, but includes counting in 2s, 5s, 10s and 100s, starting with any number and moving forwards and backwards. The patterns of numbers established in such counting can encourage the development of strategies that are powerful when they are connected to the arithmetic operations.

There are also connections to be established among the operations and links to be made with the particular numbers that appear in problems. If the reader takes time to do the three calculations: 25 + 26, 39 + 17 and 12 + 35, it will probably become clear that a different strategy is used for each one, using results and relationships that are relevant. The first may be derived quickly from the 'known fact' that 25 + 25 = 50. The second may be 'transformed' to 40 + 16 = 56 while the third is most likely to involve 'partitioning' the numbers to find 10 + 30 + 2 + 5, or some similar procedure. Applying a standard procedure would not be as efficient as this selection of appropriate strategies based on number sense.

> Number sense refers to a person's general understanding of number and operations along with the ability and inclination to use this understanding in flexible ways to make mathematical judgements and to develop useful strategies for handling numbers and operations.
>
> (McIntosh *et al.*, 1992)

According to the analysis of McIntosh *et al.* (1992) there are three key areas where number sense plays a key role:

- *knowledge of and facility with numbers* – a sense of orderliness of number; multiple representations for numbers; a sense of relative and absolute magnitude of numbers; and a system of benchmark referents for thinking about numbers;
- *knowledge of and facility with operations* – an understanding of the effects of operations; an awareness of the rules that apply; and an awareness of the relationships between the operations; and
- *applying this knowledge and facility with numbers and operations to problems requiring reasoning with numbers* – understanding the relationship between a problem context and appropriate solution strategies; awareness that multiple strategies exist; inclination to utilize an efficient representation and/or method; and an inclination to review data and results.

Knowledge of numbers involves an understanding of the structure and regularity of the number system, starting with whole numbers and extending to rational numbers (that is, those that can be represented as fractions and decimals) and the way these systems are linked. Facility with operations involves the links among them, for example doubling being the same as multiplying by 2. It includes an appreciation of certain rules and knowledge of when these can be used, for example, in addition and multiplication the numbers can be reversed so that $8 + 3$ is equal to $3 + 8$ and $8 \times 3$ is equal to $3 \times 8$. For subtraction and division, on the other hand, reversing the numbers will give different calculations with different solutions. Utilizing numerical knowledge involves an understanding of which operations to use in problem-solving, knowing when it is appropriate to work with approximations and making sense of calculation procedures and results in terms of the original problem.

Some relationships are the crucial building blocks for working with numbers and these may be identified as 'benchmarks', for example the number pairs that make 10, or the equivalence of 0.5, ½ and 50%. When presented with a new problem, whether it is in words or symbols, an effective solution strategy will involve careful consideration of the numbers involved to identify links with any facts or relationships that are already known. Number sense develops continually as the range of known facts and the relationships among them are extended. But how are in-experienced children to come to know which facts are crucial to *know* and which are easily *derived* from others? It is here that judgement differs from one individual to another and the gap in apparent ability begins to open. What has been termed the '7-year gap' in children's mathematical ability becomes evident by the top of the primary school with some 11-year-olds performing no better than average 7-year-olds, while others show the ability of average 14-year-olds (Cockcroft, 1982). It has been suggested that the term 'slow learner' with respect to mathematics is a misnomer as children who are struggling are often not identifying links and relationships, and are consequently learning more, unconnected procedures (Gray and Tall, 1994). The example used is the child who sees no connection between addition, subtraction and counting and so has three unrelated processes to master. Learning that subtraction can be achieved by counting on from the smaller number is one of the 'benchmarks' in early calculating.

## The importance of understanding

Understanding relationships between numbers, and progressively developing methods of computation, has become the focus for learning, replacing the traditional 'four rules of arithmetic' in curriculum requirements. Although the number facts to be acquired are often the same as in the past, the process of learning now involves children in constructing and refining their own methods.

> The teacher's role is not simply to accept pupils' personal methods but to help them adopt better ones. By explaining, discussing and comparing different part-written, part-mental methods [teachers] can guide pupils towards choosing and using methods that are quicker, can be applied more widely and are helpful to their future learning.
>
> (DfEE, 2001, p. 11)

Work of eminent psychologists has led teachers to recognize the need to involve pupils actively in their own learning and to focus on mathematics as a thinking process rather than a catalogue of facts and procedures to memorize. Children are no longer considered as 'passive' receivers of information, but are 'actively' involved in constructing their own knowledge through discussing their own strategies and making sense of those used by others. This is reflected in the shift from endless 'drill and practice' of standard procedures that was typical for past generations to requirements identified in the National Curriculum: *using* mathematics, *communicating* mathematically and developing mathematical *reasoning*. Explaining what they are doing and justifying their decisions helps children to develop skills in reasoning and clarity in communication that will have benefits across many aspects of learning beyond mathematics. Such developments in teaching, all of which have learning with understanding as a central requirement, reflect the views of psychologists and researchers about the most effective ways to help children learn mathematics.

A key objective for teaching is to establish learning with understanding. Understanding, however, is not easy to define and two different types of understanding have been identified with respect to mathematics. The type of understanding required to reproduce taught procedures has been called *instrumental understanding* and compared with *relational understanding* where knowledge extends from *how* to do a calculation to *why* the procedures work (Skemp, 1976). While number work in the past has been associated with tedious repetition of standard procedures, more recent trends in teaching have introduced investigational approaches and a classroom environment where the thinking of individuals is valued. For 'relational' understanding, learners are never asked to accept, but instead are asked to try developing their own meanings. Skemp proposes that relational knowledge can be a goal in itself for 'if people get satisfaction from relational understanding they may not only try to understand relationally new material which is put before them, but also actively seek out new material and explore new areas ... making what is often called the "motivational side" of a teacher's job much easier' (Skemp, 1976).

## Classroom resources that help develop imagery

Mathematical understanding involves progression from practical experiences to talking about these experiences, first using informal language, and then more formal language. Later, children will learn to use the symbols that characterize the conciseness and precision of a mathematically reasoned argument. Just as speech is transferred to writing over an extended period of time in school, with complexities arising in manipulative control and spelling, so transfer from concrete experiences to mental methods and symbolic representation takes time in mathematics.

$$\begin{bmatrix} \text{concrete} \\ \text{experiences} \end{bmatrix} \rightarrow \begin{bmatrix} \text{abstract/mental} \\ \text{methods} \end{bmatrix} \rightarrow \begin{bmatrix} \text{symbolizing} \\ \text{relations} \end{bmatrix}$$

Beginning with the manipulation of real objects, sorting and rearranging different collections, children are introduced to patterns that will be identified with number words. The number 'three', for example, can be represented as a collection of 3 buttons, or as 3 toys or 3 steps, but 'three' itself is an abstraction from each of these situations and ideas such as '3 years old' will take some time to understand. Talking about their experiences will help children establish the significance of number words that relate to the visual patterns that they consistently meet and provide the foundations for mental imagery.

Mental imagery can also be encouraged through patterns and symbols. Sometimes patterns are more evident in written form than in the spoken words, for example, starting with 13 and adding tens will result in the pattern '13, 23, 33, 43, 53, 63 ...' Here the counting pattern '1, 2, 3, 4, 5, 6 ...' appears in the first 'place' for each number and will continue '73, 83, 93, 103, 113 ...', although the words to be matched to these higher numbers give less of a clue that this pattern continues. Making patterns explicit and building connections between different visual images will help to establish relationships that exist among numbers.

Before they can operate with abstract numbers, children will learn to 'model' situations with their fingers or some form of apparatus that can represent the real objects. In the classroom, beads or cubes are introduced because they can be linked together and so have the potential to represent numbers in a structured way. Cubes are sometimes favoured because they can be used not only to model different numbers, but also to show the place value structure of the number system in 'tens' and 'units'

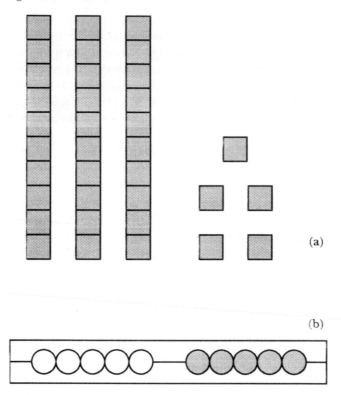

(a)

(b)

**Figure 1.1**   (a) Cubes to show 'tens' and 'units'.
(b) A bead frame and a bead string.

(Figure 1.1a). An alternative representation of numbers that relates more closely to the counting sequence involves beads that
can be joined on a 'bead frame' or in a 'bead string' (Figure 1.1b).
'Place value' and 'counting' will be seen in the chapters of this
book as alternative focuses for early work with numbers, each
identified with the development of different calculating strategies.

It is important that children do not come to rely on using such materials for modelling numbers but that they develop mental imagery associated with these materials and can work with 'imagined' situations. Research has shown that an important stage between the actual manipulation of objects and abstract work with numbers is a stage in which objects are imagined (Hughes, 1986). Although some children will progress spontaneously to using mental imagery, others may need a transitional stage in which the materials to be manipulated are covered or hidden once they have been used and the children encouraged to reproduce in their minds the procedures involved.

Classroom materials provide powerful images, not only for representing individual numbers, but also for illustrating the way numbers are related in a logical structure. Representation to focus on the ordering of numbers may be seen in various versions of the *number line* which models the counting sequence. Initially the number line may be represented by linking beads on a string, or with cubes that can be structured into a line that is sometimes referred to as a *number track* (Figure 1.2a). At this stage each item will represent a number in the counting sequence. An important development occurs when the number labels are 'attached' to the divisions between each item so that the number 12, for example, is associated with twelve complete sections (Figure 1.2b). This number line appears on rulers and scales, and experiences with measuring instruments will help to reinforce the meaning of the calibrations. Most recently, an *empty number line* has been introduced for modelling mental calculations where the number order is preserved but the intervals are not marked. Without marked intervals, numbers can be represented in a flexible way using 'jumps' to illustrate the stages in a calculation (Figure 1.2c). The empty number line is an important innovation in teaching and will be the focus for Chapter 5.

In traditional classrooms, the place value aspect of numbers has been emphasized more than counting, with images relating to 'tens sticks' and 'unit cubes' and later with *Dienes' materials* including 'hundreds blocks' and even 'thousands cubes'. Using these materials, the operations of addition and subtraction can be identified with procedures for moving around the concrete materials and related to written recording. With this imagery,

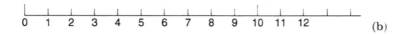

| 1 | 2 | 3 | 4 | 5 | 6 | 7 | 8 | | (a)

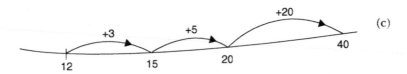

(b)

(c)

**Figure 1.2**   (a) Number track.
                 (b) Calibrated number line.
                 (c) Empty number line.

children must learn that the 'tens stick' represents at the same time '10 unit ones' and '1 unit ten'. Similarly, a single block is used to represent '1 hundred' with its equivalence to '10 tens' and '100 ones' evident in the size and structure of the materials. These materials have been closely associated with the column arithmetic that was central in the past, but today the focus on mental strategies will often relate to numbers as wholes, and more intuitive ideas based on counting. Today, even many written strategies involve whole numbers throughout, with no need to split them into tens and units.

When number symbols are familiar, their arrangement on a *100 square* (Figure 1.3a) will illustrate the regularity with which certain symbols appear and the logical structure of the symbol patterns even where the words do not clearly relate to their position (for example, eleven or twelve) (Tapson, 1995). This resource can be

| 1 | 2 | 3 | 4 | 5 | 6 | 7 | 8 | 9 | 10 |
|---|---|---|---|---|---|---|---|---|---|
| 11 | 12 | 13 | 14 | 15 | 16 | 17 | 18 | 19 | 20 |
| 21 | 22 | 23 | 24 | 25 | 26 | 27 | 28 | 29 | 30 |
| 31 | 32 | 33 | 34 | 35 | 36 | 37 | 38 | 39 | 40 |
| 41 | 42 | 43 | 44 | 45 | 46 | 47 | 48 | 49 | 50 |
| 51 | 52 | 53 | 54 | 55 | 56 | 57 | 58 | 59 | 60 |
| 61 | 62 | 63 | 64 | 65 | 66 | 67 | 68 | 69 | 70 |
| 71 | 72 | 73 | 74 | 75 | 76 | 77 | 78 | 79 | 80 |
| 81 | 82 | 83 | 84 | 85 | 86 | 87 | 88 | 89 | 90 |
| 91 | 92 | 93 | 94 | 95 | 96 | 97 | 98 | 99 | 100 |

(a)

| 1 | 2 | 3 | 4 | 5 | 6 | 7 | 8 | 9 |
|---|---|---|---|---|---|---|---|---|
| 10 | 20 | 30 | 40 | 50 | 60 | 70 | 80 | 90 |
| 100 | 200 | 300 | 400 | 500 | 600 | 700 | 800 | 900 |
| 1 000 | 2 000 | 3 000 | 4 000 | 5 000 | 6 000 | 7 000 | 8 000 | 9 000 |
| 10 000 | 20 000 | 30 000 | 40 000 | 50 000 | 60 000 | 70 000 | 80 000 | 90 000 |
| 100 000 | 200 000 | 300 000 | 400 000 | 500 000 | 600 000 | 700 000 | 800 000 | 900 000 |

(b)

**Figure 1.3** (a) 100 square.
(b) Gattegno chart.

13

used to illustrate counting on and back in ones (moving horizontally), or counting on or back in tens (moving vertically) although many children find this a source of confusion and prefer a number line to 100. An alternative representation showing number structure is presented in a *Gattegno chart* (Figure 1.3b) which focuses on the way larger numbers are constructed by identifying their constituent parts (Faux, 1998). Using the images presented in such a chart, the number symbols and the words to identify them can be brought together. Children can be encouraged to identify the representation of numbers such as 364 ('three hundred and sixty four') with 300 ('three hundred') and 60 ('sixty') and 4 ('four') and this will be influential in the mental calculating strategies that children learn. These resources can help the development of imagery to support calculating methods, particularly for addition and subtraction, and this aspect will be discussed in later chapters of this book.

## Further classroom resources

One of the most effective ways to encourage mental work and classroom discussion is through the use of games and puzzles, inside and outside the classroom. These can present further images of numbers in different structured formats and can motivate children to tackle numerous calculations in their heads. Games can stimulate children to reflect on numerical relationships in a way that encourages them to seek results and relationships that will be advantageous in their game strategy. They will draw on all their experiences with numbers in order to make sense of every situation that arises in a manner that more formal work with numbers does not always encourage. In support of games, Parr (1994) writes that 'a game can stimulate people to do willingly some quite demanding and not very attractive arithmetic'. He also notes that 'games can stimulate people to give repeated practice to skills of mental arithmetic and then do the whole thing again simply because they want to do better the second time around'. This support for games is endorsed by Hatch (1998) who suggests that games 'improve mental skills through repetition', provide children with a sense of ownership through which they become autonomous in their thinking, and develop skills in asking as well as answering questions. She notes that 'when playing a game there is pressure to work mentally' and there is encouragement to develop flexibility as 'a game does not define the way in which a problem is to be solved'. As a classroom resource they can present teachers with opportunities for listening to children – 'eavesdropping on playing games is an excellent way to assess their mental skills' and 'to identify misconceptions'. Unlike a test, the traditional method for reinforcing mental skills, games are less threatening. When playing games children's thinking can be more transparent, particularly where they are encouraged to 'think aloud' and share their strategies with others.

## Problem-solving or exploring structure

If children are to appreciate number work as a pursuit that makes sense, in addition to having appropriate images, they must be clear about the reasons for calculating. Separate learning objectives may be appropriate for different activities with numbers. Anghileri (2001a) suggests two distinct purposes for calculating: for solving individual problems and for exploring the structure of the number system. *Calculating for problem-solving* may require a 'convergent' methodology where the main aim is to find and interpret the solution to a particular problem. This will differ from the more analytical, 'divergent' approaches that are used in *calculating for exploring structure*, where the purpose is to focus on many possible approaches to a calculation in order to highlight the mathematical relationships and processes that can be involved.

- In *calculating for problem-solving* only one approach will be necessary in order to find a solution and it may not always be appropriate to debate the most succinct written method. The focus will be on interpreting the information for a given problem, modelling the situation arithmetically, and applying the result to a real solution of the problem. Division provides a good example of the way this may involve mathematical thinking, even where a calculator is used. For the problem 'How many buses are needed to transport 532 people on 15-seater buses?', initial identification of the operation as division would lead to the answer 35.466667 which would need to be interpreted in terms of the number of buses needed.

● In addition to the solution of a particular problem, experiences of *calculating for exploring structure* may involve many different ways to tackle a single calculation and discussion to assess the effectiveness of different approaches. The purpose will be to identify links among numbers, and among the operations, that will help to develop children's understanding of number relationships. An example may involve possible ways to calculate 300 − 158, and could include the relationship between addition and subtraction, and the use of 'near doubles'. Such exploration could include the use of a calculator, for example to discuss what is happening when 10 is divided by 4 or 3.

These different purposes for calculating could be combined but children need to be aware of the objectives in a particular activity and separating these two purposes may provide a clearer agenda for children's learning. Each purpose will strengthen the skills and understanding gained from the other, and the two should be seen as complementary rather than separate, just as reading and writing are related elements in learning language.

## Purposes in teaching mathematics

Wider perspectives for teaching number sense are introduced when the purposes in teaching mathematics are reviewed more generally. In discussing some of the different purposes that have been identified, Huckstep (1999) includes such utilitarian justifications for teaching mathematics as providing 'a tool in everyday life' and 'a means of communication' but also identifies its 'usefulness in providing mental training' and 'as a means for empowering people'. The first of these may be satisfied by teaching standardized procedures for calculating but the others suggest that computational skills without number sense will provide a poor educational opportunity to children. The flexibility and inventiveness identified with number sense will become established only where children are aware of the power of pure mathematical reasoning. This power has been acknowledged within ancient civilizations but most recently has led to the development of a technology that has had profound effects on society with the invention of calculators and computers. These are testament to the power of mathematical thinking that has its roots in children's earliest calculations.

All children can derive satisfaction from this mathematical thinking as they observe patterns and relationships that present connections among numbers or procedures, and teachers will be aware of the positive motivation personal 'discoveries' can nurture. Huckstep discusses mathematics 'as a source of aesthetic satisfaction and a form of entertainment'. This may be contested by adults who were subjected to 'drill and practice', where rules were learned without reason and a feeling of inadequacy was common among, perhaps, the majority of children in the classroom. He highlights mathematical thinking as 'one of the pinnacles of mankind's intellectual achievements' and this can be reflected in the pleasure that can be experienced by children who feel in control of their work with numbers.

Learning about numbers and number operations can provide opportunities to go beyond the utilitarian applications to explore patterns and relationships that can be fascinating and can lead to logical thinking and mathematical reasoning. Observation based on simple calculations can, for example, lead to predictions and justifications that illustrate the way powerful thought may be initiated. Consider the fact that when the consecutive odd numbers are added the result is a square number:

$$1 + 3 = 2 \times 2;$$
$$1 + 3 + 5 = 3 \times 3;$$
$$1 + 3 + 5 + 7 = 4 \times 4;$$
$$1 + 3 + 5 + 7 + 9 = 5 \times 5.$$

When the pattern is analysed it becomes possible to *predict* the sum of the first 10 odd numbers, or the first 1000 odd numbers, without having to calculate. Asking *why* this relationship exists invites children into the fascinating world of numbers where there are always logical explanations to be found and often intriguing facts to be explored along the way.

## Activities

1. List any calculations you have done over the past week, and identify the purposes for these calculations. Were they exact calculations or estimates? Were they written or mental?
2. What other ways have you used numbers recently?

# CHAPTER 2

# Counting and Coming to Know Numbers

Before they start school, children have a rich experience of numbers that relate to their personal lives. Some are beginning to acquire diverse understandings that will be the basis for number sense. Initially the number facts that they know will be isolated, just as new words are learned singly before they are integrated into more flowing speech. The number four, for example, can be very significant when a child's own fourth birthday is anticipated. Many children will recognize the symbol for four, associating it with the '4' they have seen on a birthday card. Understanding the relationships that exist among numbers can, however, be complex as illustrated when the child tries to understand 'now you are three and soon you will be four', as the reasons for changing age do not appear to relate to any precise physical happening.

In these early stages, some differences between numbers can also be personally significant. For example, the ages of older friends and younger siblings may be used by parents to explain a variety of phenomena, from bedtimes to allowances made for behaviour. These isolated uses of number words need to be reconciled with the logical system that is used for counting, and a variety of experiences are needed if young children are to master the sub-skills necessary to understand the ways numbers work. Experiences with objects and images will initially appear to be unrelated to the number words and symbols that they meet but connections will become more apparent through consistent use of numbers in meaningful activities.

## Cardinal and ordinal aspects of number

There are two distinct ways in which numbers relate to sets of objects and these are referred to as the *cardinal* and the *ordinal* aspects of a number. A number is used in one sense to denote the size of a set and children will gradually come to recognize the common characteristic in, for example *four* candles, *four* wheels and *four* sweets. Where objects in one set can be placed alongside objects in another, the practical experiences of matching will help children identify one meaning of the number word 'four' as the quantity in each of the sets. This identification of a number word with the quantity in a set is referred to as the *cardinal* (or *quantity*) aspect of number and involves skills in matching and pattern recognition as children use the number words *two, three* and *four* before they identify them within the structure of the counting system. The tactile experiences of moving objects around and perhaps lining them up alongside each other will reinforce the sameness in quantity in a way that is not possible if static images alone are used. Where the context gives a meaning for this matching activity, children will understand the purpose more readily than the abstract tasks that are found on worksheets in a classroom; for example, *three* bears, *three* bowls, *three* spoons, *three* chairs and *three* beds in the story of Goldilocks.

A different use of number words occurs when they locate a position in the counting sequence. For example, a child might count steps on the way to bed 'one, two, three, four ...' In this case the word *four* is uttered after *three* and before *five*, and refers to the *fourth* step from the beginning rather than the collection of the first four steps together. The identification of a number with its position in a sequence is referred to as the *ordinal* (or *location*) aspect of number. In order to count in this way it is necessary not only to know the correct sequence of number words, but also to coordinate this in a one-to-one correspondence with the objects being counted, memorizing those that have already been counted and those that remain.

## Importance of counting for explaining numbers

To appreciate the connection between a sequence of number words and a collection of objects requires a combination of verbal, visual and tactile experiences which all give cognitive cues about the process of counting. Nunes and Bryant describe counting as 'a system which is partly an expression of universal laws and partly a bundle of convenient but arbitrary conventions' (Nunes and Bryant, 1996, p. 22). In order to identify some of the complexities which arise they note that the naming of numbers has a 'place-value' structure which does not become clear until the larger number names are reached. The name for 'fifty-three' probably makes more sense as 'five tens and three units' than 'eleven' which is difficult to identify as 'one ten and one unit'. In their early experiences children have to memorize a large collection of names and images. Only later will these be pieced together to reveal the underlying logical structure.

Much like early language learning, counting develops through a process in which the child can often take the initiative and a little encouragement will help to establish some of the basic knowledge upon which counting is built. Penny Munn (1997) talks of 'multiple overlapping developments in verbal, motor and cognitive activities that become integrated with each other over time'. She proposes that children's *beliefs* about counting are central to their development and discusses intervention activities which can lead young children into counting. Such activities involve:

- taking young children's counting seriously even when it is purely verbal and does not appear to have a purpose;
- stimulating children to develop their own numerical goals and use counting in relation to their personal lives;
- making the purpose of counting explicit to children; and
- assessing children's beliefs about counting before comparing sets or working on adding and subtracting.

She notes that 'it is not until children acquire some experience of the mental activities involved in other people's counting' that they are able to 'internalize the cultural practice of counting' (Munn, 1997, p. 18).

## Learning to count

There are many skills to be acquired on the way to mastering counting and a rich network of connections are needed that cannot be *given* to children but must be learned through experiences in the real world and then expressed in the formal language and symbols of mathematics. Because counting is a powerful unifying idea in early number work, several research studies have analysed the stages of learning and the skills that are integrated in being able to count 'properly'. From pre-counting experiences with words that relate to quantities through to the coordination of hand, eye, memory and cognitive schema for recording numerical data, there is the potential for confusion if support is not available for children to 'test out' their developing ideas about numbers. The involvement of an interested adult or an older child who is willing to engage in discussions about numbers will give a head start to those learning to count.

## Pre-counting experiences

Very young children will develop an understanding of *pre-number* ideas; for example the word 'more' is often used with confidence when quantities are increased. It has been shown that young children of two and three years exhibit number sense where they are able to distinguish sets of two or three items although they may not yet know the number words to describe such sets (Gelman and Gallistel, 1978). When children were shown a plate with three mice and the same plate with one mouse surreptitiously removed, they looked around and under the plate showing that they knew one was missing even though they did not have words to describe what had happened. At this stage the number names have little meaning and it will be some time before isolated number words are associated with an ordering of quantities. By asking three- and four-year-olds if they would prefer *five* sweets or *three* sweets (or other such pairs of numbers) the same researchers assessed children's understanding of the number words and found that they were unable to compare two sets by the number words alone.

## Meaningful contexts

Children can, however, begin to operate logically with numbers from an early age, and Martin Hughes (1986) shows how they can display sound understanding of numerical relationships when there is a meaningful context. He documents children's difficulties working with abstract questions but shows that the same problems could be solved when set in real situations. In one task, three cubes were placed in a tin and shown to the children. When one was then taken out, without seeing inside the tin even three-year-olds knew that there were two cubes left but became confused when asked the question 'what is three take away one?' He compared children's responses to real and abstract tasks and concluded that it is not always their number sense that is being tested. Where children were given a situation that they could think about in order to give meaning to a numerical question they were able to make sense of the question. Even where the situation was an imagined one, their success rates were higher than for purely abstract problems. This has implications for the classroom as the move from real experiences to abstract thinking can present great difficulties for some children. Children need to progress from practical experiences to working with imagery of those experiences and they will also need to identify for themselves appropriate images for tackling different problems. Later chapters will discuss the way in which calculation strategies can be developed using different visual imagery.

## Stages and progression

Counting is a complex process involving many sub-skills and it takes children a considerable time to become competent. Learning to count takes place in a social environment, so parents and carers are the first 'teachers' introducing ideas involving numbers. They will not plan a progressive programme but may, quite naturally, involve children in reciting the counting sequence through games, rhymes and stories. This is an important part of a child's experience as reciting number sequences is a basic skill needed for counting. Memorizing rhymes and songs can provide a child's first experiences of counting forwards and backwards and using many different rhymes will help to establish consistency in ordering number words.

At the same time there are other skills that researchers have associated with 'stages' in the development of number and Schaeffer et al. (1974) characterize three stages that mark children's developing understanding of number:

- 'Stage One' children can understand the meaning of 'more' (but not 'less'), they can discriminate between small numbers on the basis of their perceptual patterns and can distinguish between larger and smaller collections provided they are lined up to show a 1–1 correspondence;

- '*Stage Two*' children can determine numbers from one to four by recognition or counting but for larger numbers their counting becomes inaccurate with difficulties coordinating speech with counting. They may understand the cardinal aspect for very small collections but have not yet related the two aspects for numbers greater than four;

- '*Stage Three*' children are reasonably accurate counting up to ten and are beginning to connect the count for any set (the ordinal aspect) with the number that represents the whole collection (the cardinal aspect). They can use a count to find the size of a collection but cannot compare collections by their number name only.

Dickson, Brown and Gibson (1984) discuss these stages in detail in their review of such research and conclude that 'the child has to construct for himself the connection between the recitation of arbitrary sounds and the size of a collection'. Making sense of numbers involves the integration of many skills that develop from children's practical experiences with numbers.

## Small number pattern recognition

Through everyday activities children can gain experience of sorting and comparing collections of objects and some will appreciate certain patterns that help to distinguish one set from another. Particularly notable are those associations that can be made with the children themselves. For example, 'two' can be identified with one in each hand and an extra one may lead to the notion of 'three'. The spatial arrangements for one, two and three are recognized earliest, then four objects arranged in a square – and one in the centre makes five, just like the dots on a dice. It is common for children to recognize five as it appears on a dice but not when objects are arranged as a row of three together with a row of two. This is an example of a situation where the re-arrangement of objects will help children to understand that the same number word applies so long as no more objects are added and none are taken away. Later, the representation of five as a set of fingers on one hand (and ten as two hands) will be important for supporting calculating strategies. Talking about these arrangements with friends or an adult will help children to develop strategies for rearranging and recognizing quantities and for using early number language. However, without appropriate interactions the activities can remain meaningless. When patterns or special arrangements of objects are instantly recognized this skill is called *subitizing*. There is no counting involved but a spatial arrangement becomes familiar and it is consistently associated with the same number word.

## *Matching in a one-to-one correspondence*

Sets can be compared by making a *one-to-one correspondence* between the objects in the sets to see which has the greater number (Figure 2.1a). The activity of lining up objects in rows or towers to make a comparison involves checking that both have the same 'starting point' from which the quantities will be viewed. Notions of more and fewer/less will be identified with which line is longest or which tower is tallest. At the same time, children may be misled by physical characteristics like the image presented when a row of small objects appears shorter than a longer row of large objects although the number in each row may be the same. Children will believe that the spatial arrangement of a collection can affect the quantity and that a collection has more in it when it is spread out (Figure 2.1b).

Piaget (1965) identified '*conservation*' as the concept that enables children to realize that quantity is not affected by any rearrangement and he demonstrated that young children are frequently misled by their intuitive judgements. In his classic experiments, when two rows of objects were *matched* young children appreciated that there was the same quantity in each but when one of the rows was spread out or brought together they thought the rows no longer had the same quantity of items.

Many researchers have replicated Piaget's tests and show that in the early stages even children who can count do not make their judgement by counting but use perceptual judgements and may easily be misled. Fuson (1988) designed some experiments that

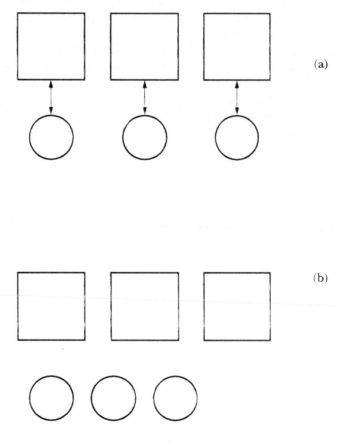

(a)

(b)

**Figure 2.1**  (a)  Matching in a *one-to-one correspondence*.
(b)  A row of small objects may appear to be less than a longer row of large objects.

attempted to lead children to use other than perceptual strategies by colour-matching the objects in two sets and first comparing sets where there were no misleading cues, for example. She showed that four- and five-year-olds still relied on misleading length cues when comparing the sizes of two sets even when they could obtain information by counting.

## *The cardinality principle – naming a collection*

In a progression in the skills that children acquire on the way to effective counting, the early skill of *pattern recognition* (which is developed in children as young as two years old) is followed much later by the skill to give a number name to a collection. When children start counting collections of objects they point to items one at a time and are most likely to be unaware that the single number word that ends the count represents the totality of the collection. This recognition and ability to name the whole set is called the *cardinality principle*. The words that are used to identify different sub-skills are not important, but the knowledge that there is a step in transferring from counting in ones to this use of numbers to designate a whole collection may explain why some children appear to be slow in progressing with their number work. To combine '3' and '2' in any form of addition will be difficult if the '3' is associated only with an individual object (the one that is pointed at as the word 'three' is uttered) and not with the whole collection of three objects.

A *skill integrationist* perspective on the way children learn is proposed by Schaeffer *et al.* (1974) as they suggest how the ability to count effectively develops over a period of time. By recognizing the spatial arrangement for naming a collection of two or three objects, and identifying this with the verbal count for a one-to-one correspondence, children are able to deduce that the last counting word is the name given to the collection. With the ability to recognize a pattern for four or five objects, an association with the longer counting sequence is made and so the mental connection is made between the 'name' for the last object and the 'name' for the whole set. By making logical deductions and testing their own thinking, children will begin to experience the underlying structures that unify counting and number patterns. It is at this stage that number sense begins to develop as they come to understand the different roles that numbers and number words can play.

Other researchers have identified a transition that is evident when the ordinal and the cardinal aspect of numbers come to be related in children's thinking. Steffe *et al.* (1983) refer to a transfer that is made from the *component* nature of numbers to their *composite* nature. Pupils also need to progress from understanding a 'unit' as a single object (a singleton unit) and a 'unit' as a group of objects (a composite unit) (Schools Curriculum and Assesment Authority, 1997). Understanding that 'ten' can be both ten individual items and at the same time a 'ten' that is counted as 'one ten' is necessary for understanding place value. Until this distinction is understood, progress in calculating cannot be made. Making these links between the different uses of numbers and counting will give children powerful mental strategies for problem-solving and these will be explored further in later chapters.

## Abstraction principle – what can be counted

In identifying the procedures that need to be mastered in early counting Gelman and Gallistel (1978) propose the *abstraction principle* that deals with the definition of what is countable. The range of entities that children perceive to be countable increases with experience but is often not as limited as school schemes may indicate (many things can be counted – seen or unseen, sounds, movements, 'pairs!', hundreds and quarters). What children can count is often related to their personal pre-school experiences, for example Ellie (four years two months), who lives opposite a church with a clock that chimes the hour, has learned to count the chimes because she understands the relevance certain times have for her daily routine. In their research Gelman and Gallistel found that pre-school children could count diverse and hetero-geneous sets (for example, assorted trinkets and shells) and their accuracy seems to be unaffected by the introduction of diverse materials. They conclude that 'young children can readily group a variety of two-dimensional and three-dimensional materials under the rubric of "things to be counted" '.

The idea of what children can count has been developed further by Steffe *et al.* (1983) who identify five different types of countable item of progressive difficulty:

- *perceptual* units: items that can be identified as discrete 'things' to be counted as children would count a collection of buttons;
- *figural* units: items that are not immediately available but are

recalled and imagined (for example, the pets a child has at home);

- *motor* units: items that are motor acts like pointing, or movements like steps;
- *verbal* units: utterances like number words that can themselves be counted (for example, saying '8, 9, 10' and knowing three numbers had been counted); and
- *abstract* units: items that can be introduced by the child to 'match' the count for any given number.

This progression takes children from seeing, touching and counting 'actual' objects to understanding that the abstract number itself may be identified with the count that generates it (for example 'eight' by itself implies the sequence 'one, two, ... eight'). School experiences are too often limited to static collections on workcards and some children fail to develop to the level of abstraction that is necessary to operate effectively with numbers.

### Order-irrelevance principle

The *order-irrelevance principle* 'captures the way' different skills 'interact in contributing to a full appreciation of what counting is about' (Gelman and Gallistel, 1978, p. 141). Number tags can be given to any of the objects as long as there is one for each and all objects are included. It does not matter which number tag is assigned to which item and the count can 'jump around' to attach the numbers in order to the items. This principle is demonstrated when moving objects, for example fish in a tank or children in a playground, are to be counted and it may take several attempts to complete the task with different starting points and different strategies for keeping track.

### Summarizing the stages

By understanding the stages in learning to count and the range of skills to be mastered, teachers can monitor progress and provide activities that will address particular sub-skills that are not yet well established. The stages of learning to count have been summarized by Thompson as follows:

- *recitation*: being able to recite the number words in their correct sequence;
- *enumeration*: assigning the correctly ordered number words in one-to-one correspondence with the objects being counted; and
- *cardinality*: realizing that the number assigned to the final object counted tells how many there are in the whole collection.

Thompson goes on to identify activities that will help children to develop the individual skills and notes that 'only when children can successfully satisfy all three ... criteria can it be said they are able to count' (Thompson, 1997, p. 131).

In supporting the view that there are many diverse skills that children will only master over an extended period of time, Nunes and Bryant refer to a variety of researchers' experiments where the results suggest that children initially learn to count without understanding that counting is a measure of set size. They conclude that 'it is one thing to be able to count and answer the question "how many?" but quite another to understand the significance of the number uttered at the end of counting as a measure of set size' (Nunes and Bryant, 1996, p. 41).

## Developing counting skills

When children start school many are skilled counters (some in a more limited sense than others) but they traditionally spend some time in school with 'pre-number' activities like matching, ordering and colouring which they cannot easily relate to their existing knowledge. Although such skills need to be developed in children's school experiences, their use may be better related to classifying shapes in mathematics or to science activities where the consequent outcomes can be associated with establishing relevant characteristics of objects, fruits or animals, for example. It is questionable whether the associated activities are adding to the children's number understanding and they can serve to detach school work from the useful purposes of numbers (Whitebread, 1999). Thompson (1997) questions whether there is a transfer of learning from such activities to situations involving numbers. His book *Teaching and Learning Early Number* is based on the principle that counting should be the fundamental mathematical process that needs to be addressed from the child's earliest experiences in school.

As well as learning to recognize some small number patterns, children in school can start by reciting number words as a social activity that reinforces the universal nature of counting. Together they can begin to enjoy the stability of the counting sequence, acquiring rhythm and pace as they develop a feeling for verbal patterns. This play with words should be encouraged as similar patterns and rhythms underpin many mathematical strategies in later problem-solving. Such apparently simple rhymes as 'One, two, three, Mother caught a flea ...', for example, have a rhythm that may be developed to 'one, two, *three*, four, five, *six*, ...' as a pre-requisite pattern for learning the facts for multiplication by three (Anghileri, 1997).

## Introducing resources to develop mental imagery

In addition to developing verbal skills in counting, children will use visual imagery to help them establish the patterns and relationships that exist within the counting sequence. A 'bead frame' or 'bead string' of ten beads made up of two sets of five beads in different colours serves as an introduction to the numbered line that is one of the most useful images for relating numbers and counting. Counting along the line of beads will provide further visual images of numbers that reflect the relationships that exist, for example that six is one more than five, and each child can have a personal 'bead string' of ten beads to organize and re-organize. As well as relating the images to the counting sequence, the arrangements generated by 'splitting' the beads into two sets can illustrate all the number pairs that make ten. The ideas and images relate well to the ten fingers that are arranged on two hands which also provide an invaluable resource for developing imagery for the number relationships that can be found in a set of ten.

## Number bonds in ten

The number pairs that together combine to make ten can be memorized to provide important 'benchmarks' as known facts from which other combinations can be derived. There are many games and puzzles available that are based on the pairs of numbers that together make ten. Initially some form of images will be important for checking and children can be encouraged to talk about the numbers that relate in this way. Some puzzles have a self-checking element involving coordinated colours or interlocking pieces so that children can play on their own. The intention is to give children instant recall of numbers that together make ten and also to develop their understanding of the links that exist between the numbers. From '5 and 5 make 10', for example, they can be encouraged to shift one across to make '4 and 6' so that the facts are not isolated. Although some children learn the relationships for themselves, when they realize their significance visual images will be helpful and all children will benefit from teacher interventions to highlight these important connections.

## Working beyond ten

Counting beyond ten will initially rely on memory as the number names between ten and 20 do not follow a clear pattern. A lot of experience will be needed before children can count reliably across boundaries such as 19, 20 ... 29, 30 ... but 99, 100 has its own appeal and is often quickly remembered. When working orally it can be fun to count 'one hundred, two hundred, three hundred ...' as the pattern here is easier to understand.

Later, children need images that can be associated with the counting sequence beyond ten. Images can be provided with a bead string of 100 beads in two colours arranged in tens, with a number line that 'grows' around the classroom, or with a 100 square where the numbers are arranged to show their place value structure (Tapson, 1995). Counting together a large collection of buttons or cubes and arranging them in groups of ten as you go can help illustrate the base ten structure of our number system, but it will take some time for children to appreciate that ten single items can also be considered as one ten for counting.

Money can also provide a helpful image when children appreciate that ten 1p coins have the same value as one 10p coin. A classroom shop or a cake sale can provide real opportunities for using 10p coins and 1p coins to make different totals. It is advisable to use real coins rather than plastic imitations as the characteristics (weight and feel) are quite different, and real coins are better related to experiences outside school. When children have experiences of counting in tens and ones in context, they can move on to the more abstract representations of the number line with the decade numbers emphasized. Later, they can mark their own numbers on an empty number line, first identifying positions for the decade numbers, and then locating other numbers around them.

## Developing flexibility in counting

The unitary counting sequence, counting in ones, starts as a list of numbers that can be recited in a particular order and once children are confident to start at one they can be encouraged to start at any number. Counting that starts, for example, at the number seven is more demanding than starting at one as it is rather like trying to complete the lines of a song or poem but starting in the middle. When children meet addition this will be an essential skill as 'counting on' is one of the effective strategies in the early stages. Even where the counting sequence can be recited, 'double counting' will be needed to keep track when 'counting on' is used. To calculate 8 + 3, for example, by saying 'eight, *nine, ten, eleven*' requires the words '*nine, ten, eleven*' to be matched with a count of three. Using fingers, tapping, nodding the head or some other physical movement may be helpful to keep track of the three number words used to count beyond eight. Some children start by finding it useful to 'put the first number in their head' and count on using fingers.

Subtraction can involve counting backwards and this needs to be practised by asking for a particular number of steps which will also require children to maintain two counts at the same time. To calculate 8 − 3 involves starting at eight and counting back three 'steps': '8 – 7, 6, 5'. This time one of the counts is backwards (7, 6,

**Figure 2.2** Calculating 8 − 3 on a number line.

5) while the other is a mental count forwards (1, 2, 3) to keep track. Again, fingers can be used to help keep track or a number line can be used to model the steps (Figure 2.2).

When multiplication is linked to counting, a triple count is necessary. Two counts relate to the individual items: one count matches a counting word with each item, while a second count monitors the fact that every set has the same number of elements.

'1, 2, 3 ... 4, 5, 6 ... 7, 8, 9 ...'
1, 2, 3    1, 2, 3    1, 2, 3

A third count is necessary to 'tally' the number of sets that have been accounted for (Anghileri, 1995a, 1997).

*Extending counting patterns*

As well as counting in ones, children can enjoy other number patterns such as counting in 2s, 3s, 5s and 10s. Although these different counts will initially be lists of numbers with little meaning, the way in which they are constructed will familiarize children with the systematic patterns that underlie some important mathematical structures such as the multiplication facts. There will be opportunities for *generalizing* the rules as they extend for themselves a count such as '5, 10, 15, 20, 25 ...', identifying which number comes next. This can introduce the challenge of extending the patterns beyond 100 which will help to reinforce understanding of the way numbers are constructed.

By learning the patterns for different numbers children can become familiar with 'nice' numbers such as 12 or 36 that appear frequently and 'not so nice' numbers, such as 13 or 23, which appear rarely. The reader will recognize that 13 and 23 are prime numbers that have no factors (other than themselves and 1) but such definitions will only appear later in school. The benefit of working with number patterns and different counting sequences is that children develop a 'feel' for numbers that will have positive benefits in helping their later calculating skills.

## Activities

1. Start to make a list of all the rhymes, songs and stories that involve numbers and counting. Add to this collection as you find new ones and share these with others.
2. With a simple four function calculator press the buttons '1, +, +' and then watch the display as you repeatedly press the equals sign. Look at what happens when you press '5, +, +' and then '=, =, =, ...' These operations can help support young children's counting as they learn to predict and check the patterns.

# CHAPTER 3

# Towards a System of Symbols

In the same way that children's early writing does not reflect their ability with words, recorded work with numbers cannot represent the mathematical thinking that they have mastered. The practice children get in forming symbols will not add to their understanding initially but will give them the conventions they need for communicating ideas in writing. For this reason it is important that they continue to develop mental strategies and that much of their mathematical thinking throughout primary school takes place through oral work. The stimulus for working with numbers can be a real problem and children enjoy any ideas that relate to their personal lives. Alternatively, the starting point can be puzzles and games that help them recognize the symbols and begin to appreciate the ordering and relationships that are important.

Activities that generate written recording need to make purposeful use of children's own recording, for example where 'cards' are made by the children themselves for matching or memory games. Price labels for a classroom shop or lists of prices for a café can be made and then sorted and re-sorted for use in many types of display. In practising to read and write numerals, children can be involved in activities that reflect the usefulness of numbers and this will motivate them to ask questions and talk about relationships.

## Symbols for numbers

In learning the symbols to represent numbers, associations are made with many different situations in which these numbers are used but children will also need to understand the more abstract nature of a number. Gray and Tall (1994) introduce the term 'procept' to try to explain certain ambiguities that exists when symbols are introduced to represent mathematical *concepts* and the *processes* involved in developing these concepts.

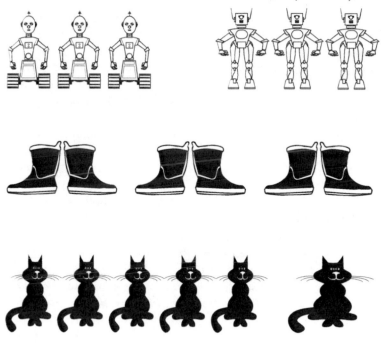

**Figure 3.1** Different images of 'six'.

Understanding 'six' includes the various ways six may be decomposed and recomposed and many of these ideas will be evident in pictorial representation of six objects where the pattern can be seen in different ways. Gray and Tall suggest that the procept 'six' includes the process of counting six and at the same time a growing collection of other representations such as 'three and three', 'three lots of two', 'one more than five' and so on (Figure 3.1).

The more varied the patterns that children can readily associate with the symbol 6, the better will be their preparation for incorporating these ideas into problem-solving strategies. Gray and Tall believe that 'ambiguity in interpreting symbolism in this flexible way is at the root of successful mathematical thinking' and they 'regard a symbol as something that is perceived by the senses. It can be written or spoken so that it can be seen or heard.' What

37

is interesting is the way symbols are interpreted differently by individuals or by the same individual at different times. Some children appear confused because they are unsure of the convention that applies in a particular situation. Reading 23, for example, as 'twenty-three' rather than 'two, three' is a convention in the same way that reading 2.30 as 'two-thirty' is a convention associated with time.

In later number work, the ideas needed for 'reading' decimal numbers may cause confusion for some children as understanding will often involve the relationships that are implicit in the number system. The decimal '0.25' is read as 'nought point two five' but it represents 25 hundredths and half of 0.5. These associations are more useful than knowing that 0.25 is 'two-tenths and five-hundredths' although this would be the extension of place value ideas to numbers less than one. Some children are not helped by their familiarity with such decimals for symbolizing money. The use of £1.25 to represent 'one pound and twenty-five pence' leaves them with a notion that five represents the 'units' in this sum. The inclusion of zero, as in 1.04, is also a source of confusion and some children find this number difficult to distinguish from 1.4.

The nature and levels of development of a procept are dependent on the cognitive growth and experiences of the child. Just as the number three may at first be associated with birthdays and candles, as the child acquires more experiences it is associated with 'the number before four' and 'half of six'. The words used for ten, eleven, twelve and so on give no clues to their representation. Children will take time to understand the way larger numbers are constructed using a place value system with ten basic symbols – 0, 1, 2, 3, 4, 5, 6, 7, 8 and 9. This is a sophisticated system as all of the millions of different numbers that are used can be constructed from the same symbols placed in different positions, for example, '23' is different from '32' and '.23' is different again.

Children have to learn to 'read' numbers like 32 and to understand what they can mean, just as they have to learn to read and interpret words in different ways in their language learning, depending on the context. Fuson *et al.* (1997) describes 'three correct conceptions' of numbers used by children:

- *unitary conception*, related to counting in ones up to 32;
- *sequencing conception*, related to counting by tens and then by ones – 10, 20, 30, 31, 32; and
- *separate tens and ones* – 1 ten, 2 tens, 3 tens and 1 unit, 2 units.

Images associated with *sequence* conception include the number line or 'jumps on the empty number line' (Beishuizen, 1999; Menne, 2001). *Separate tens and ones* are more readily associated with structured materials such as sticks of ten multilink cubes and separate cubes, or Dienes type 'tens rods' and 'unit cubes'. Difficulty in understanding the need for distinction between these two interpretations becomes clearer when the assessment question 'How many tens in 43?' is incorrectly answered '40'. Such a response would suggest that pupils have some understanding of the idea of tens but have not yet made the transition from 'unit' as 'one' and 'unit' as 'group' (in this case a 'ten') (SCAA, 1997). Fuson describes another view of numbers as a '*concatenated single-digit conception*' in which the number is thought of as two separate digits, 'three two', and associates this notion with premature introduction of column arithmetic involving 'tens and units'. Advice from the Schools Curriculum and Assessment Authority (SCAA) in the UK talks about the importance of the idea of a 'unit' and the way a collection of ten units itself becomes a 'unit ten' for calculating and for recording.

Research in the UK has shown that, even at secondary school, many pupils still have difficulties with understanding place value (Brown, 1981). One of the questions involved a meter that counts the people going into a football stand showing:

| 0 | 6 | 3 | 9 | 9 |

and pupils were asked to show the meter after *one* more person has gone in:

|  |  |  |  |  |

This was answered correctly by 68% of 12-year-olds (88% of 15-year-olds). A correct response depends on understanding the way numbers are constructed and working with such large numbers continues to be challenging to older children.

## Language difficulties

Language is central in learning about numbers and understanding at all stages will be influenced by the words that are used in discussions, questioning and explanations. Although many children readily relate their growing understanding of numbers to symbolic representation, the formalization of words and symbols may present difficulties where ambiguities are not explored. Some research analysing learning difficulties has taken as a major focus the irregularities in English words for two-digit numbers (Fuson *et al.*, 1997). Patterns are most easily seen in the larger numbers, for example, six thousand eight hundred, but the teens (thirteen, fourteen, fifteen) and early decade numbers (ten, twenty, thirty) do not conform to the regular pattern of 'number of tens' and 'number of units' (for example, sixty-four: six tens and four units). The words 'eleven' and 'twelve' bear little relationship to the 'one ten and one' and 'one ten and two' that are used to symbolize them. Even where the words are regular, confusion may arise from the abbreviated format of the symbols and a common error is for children to record 'thirty-two' literally as 302. Resources such as 'arrow cards' can be introduced to show how numbers are constructed (Figure 3.2).

The number words themselves and the symbols we use provide a shorthand representation in which numerical relationships are implicit. Traditional teaching in many countries has emphasized the place value aspect of notation, splitting numbers into 'tens' and 'units'. The emphasis on being able to say that there are '6' tens in 62 may be helpful in speedy written vertical calculations and the emphasis on teaching standard algorithms has justified this approach in the past. In schools today vertical recording is not the central way of recording calculations. If such methods are introduced before pupils can carry out calculations mentally this can hinder the development of mental strategies and lead to misunderstandings and mistakes (Fuson, 1992).

Research suggests that undue emphasis on the place value structure may invite a *digitwise* approach to calculating which will generate many errors. Instead of concentrating only on partitioning numbers into their constituent 'tens' and 'ones', understanding the structure of whole numbers may be helped by

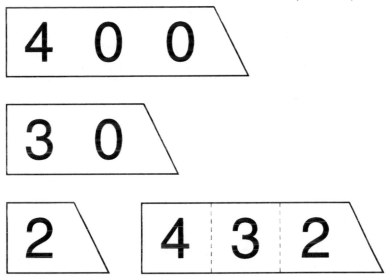

**Figure 3.2** Arrow cards to show how numbers are constructed.

partitioning numbers in a variety of ways. 'For example, being taught to treat 62 as 60 and 2, or 50 and 12, or 70 less 8', according to the different contexts in which the number is used, 'may provide a better understanding of number structure and help pupils develop effective mental strategies.' (SCAA, 1997, p. 8). This approach is sometimes identified as a *holistic* approach in which numbers are kept as wholes in any partition. Once again, the use of real examples will help illustrate the importance of different partitions: 60 seconds and 2 more; 50 pence and 12 more; 8 centimetres short of 70 centimetres.

As well as the place value partition of a number, it is important to introduce 'chunking' in a variety of ways. As well as being 30 and 6, 36 is 32 + 4 or 20 + 16 – and different 'chunks' may be associated with addition and subtraction, or with multiplication and division. The choice of partition can be crucial in finding the most efficient way to perform a calculation, as an example for calculating 1256 ÷ 6 shows (Figure 3.3).

For larger numbers such as 1256 it becomes important for children to recognize that place values may be expressed differently as 125 tens or 12 hundreds and 56. Seeing that 1256 is not

41

1256 apples are divided among 6 shopkeepers.
How many apples will every shopkeeper get?
How many apples will be left?

---

Working:    $100 \times 6 = 600$                    Answer: 1.36....

$$1000 \div 6 = 106 r 2$$
$$200 \div 6 = \cancel{480} \cancel{480} \cancel{18/20} \cancel{198} 2/r2$$
$$50 \div 6 = 8r2$$
$$6 \div 6 = 1$$

$$106 + 21 + 8 + 1 = 136$$
$$2 + 2 + 2 = 6$$

**Figure 3.3**   Calculating $1256 \div 6$.

only 1000 + 200 + 50 + 6 but also 1200 + 56 would have made the calculation so much easier.

## Looking for patterns

By working with written symbols, the logical structure of numbers will become more apparent, and patterns in the way numbers are 'built' may be related to visual imagery based on different class-room resources. The process of adding ten to any number, for example, can be illustrated on a 100 square by 'moving down' a row. Alternatively, working with 10p and 1p coins can show how a 10p coin added to 32p (three 10p and one 2p) will result in 42p (four 10p and one 2p). As an explicit illustration of the ways in which numbers are built, Gattegno charts can be used to practise naming and representing numbers with whole classes. Faux (1998) describes routines such as pointing to 800 on the chart as the children chant 'eight hundred' and then 50 as they say 'fifty' and then 3 as they say 'three'. In this way the words 'eight hundred and fifty three' may be associated with 853 as well as with 800 and 50 and 3.

Another practical teaching approach has been to 'model' the number system using cubes and rods. Such models emphasize the 'unit' ten structure with sticks of 'tens' that can be handled as a single unit. These are designed to encourage 4 as the accepted answer to 'How many tens in 45?' but children's ability to transfer from understanding the models to seeing how these 'represent' the structure and the way to manipulate numbers is questionable. Hart (1989) concluded that the manipulation of blocks to illustrate the algorithm for subtraction was not effective as 'the gap between the two types of experience is too large' and pupils saw little connection. 'The phenomenon is that children may show the ability to add numbers higher than ten when dealing with blocks or coins but seem to lose it in the transfer to symbolic notation.'

Building connections between the variety of visual imagery that is available and the abstract relationships that exist among numbers will also help children to develop the strategies they will need for calculating. In addition to jumps of ten on a number line, working with missing numbers in a hundred square can be related to adding and subtracting tens and multiples of ten (Figure 3.4).

This idea can also be related to jumps of eleven or nine on the number line and adding a 'tens stick' when working with place value materials as connections are made between the numbers and between the different images.

## Symbols for operations

As well as symbols for numbers, children have to learn to use curtailed recording that involves symbols for operations and for processes in calculating. In the early years, recording will relate to results that the children have found out by their active involvement in practical tasks, or will help in identifying patterns with numbers.

| ? | 27 | ? |
|---|----|---|
| 36 | 37 | 38 |
| ? | ? | 48 |

**Figure 3.4** Missing numbers on part of a 100 square.

Progression in learning may be summarized as:

DOING ... TALKING ABOUT ... WRITING ABOUT ... SYMBOLIZING

Written recording will begin with pictorial representations that closely relate to the images presented by materials, and gradually the images will be replaced by appropriate mathematical symbols.

Over-simplification in the use and interpretation of symbols like the operation signs '+, −, ×, ÷' or the equals sign '=' may appear to be effective in the short term since replacing words with symbols requires less well-developed manipulative skills, but on the other hand will certainly lead to limited interpretation and may lead to later confusion. For example, the subtraction symbol '−' has many interpretations including 'take away', 'subtract', 'minus', 'difference between', and may be used to represent problems of 'fewer than' or 'less than'.

Traditionally the symbols for addition and subtraction have been introduced early in a child's school experience and the teacher's role has been to explain their meaning and to instruct children in procedures for carrying out calculations. Although most children have readily adapted to the 'codes' implicit in these symbolic manipulations, the need to offer simple explanations in the early stages has led to difficulties when more complex meanings have been associated with the symbols. As an example, the idea of 'take away' as the interpretation for the subtraction symbol has led to uncertainty about 'difference' problems where comparison, rather than removal of object, is required. (For example, Tom is 6 years old and Amy is 8. What is the difference in their ages?) Current recommendations propose that 'oral and mental competence' is established 'before written calculation methods are introduced' (DfEE, 1998, p. 51). This does not mean that there will be no written recording but that children will learn to record their thinking with progressive formalization, learning first to use words to record results they can already talk about. This should include discussions about the way they themselves and their peers could record their findings with symbols introduced as a shorthand for the words they are using.

In addition to the traditional format of sums, the symbols for addition and subtraction can be used in flexible ways. Arrows are useful as they do not require the 'equals' symbols which can add complications in interpreting written statements such as: 5 = 3 + 2:

$$(3 \text{ and } 2) \xrightarrow{\text{together make}} 5$$

The symbolic statement 3 + 2 represents both the process of adding, whether through the image of physical objects or a counting pattern, and the concept of the sum that is the answer to the calculation and is another example of the procepts identified by Gray and Tall (1994). Understanding 3 + 2 = 5 involves interpreting the symbols, and understanding the concepts of 'add' and 'equals' and the processes associated with finding a solution.

Research has shown that more successful children use symbols both as objects to be manipulated and as triggers to evoke mathematical processes, with flexible ways to interpret the mathematical symbols and the numbers themselves (Anghileri, 1999). Take the mental strategy of 'near doubles' identified in the *Framework for Teaching Mathematics from Reception to Year 6* (DfEE, 1999) and the particular example 6 + 5. This becomes an easy calculation using the known fact that 5 + 5 makes 10 only if 6 is associated readily with 5 and 1 more. An equally efficient approach could be to recall the number bonds of 10 where 6 + 4 is a readily recalled total. Again, this can only be useful if 5 is associated with 4 and 1 more. This flexible use of symbols is developed alongside early recording where the pace allows discussion alongside the practising of manipulative skills.

A calculator can be a valuable additional aid to help children relate number symbols to words and to practical applications involving all kinds of numbers. As well as motivating children to think about symbols, they can provide a personal, self-correcting aid to learning about patterns and sequences of numbers. With a simple 'four function' calculator, keying in '1', '+', '+' then repeatedly '=' ..., automatically generates the counting sequence which can be used to keep a tally of anything that is being counted, while '2', '+', '+' will get the calculator counting in 2s. At a more advanced stage, ask the question, 'Will the calculator show 100 when it counts in 3s?' and you have the type of investigation that can provoke thinking about the numbers that are multiples of 3 and why 100 is not there. Early use of more powerful graphics calculators can have the advantage of showing the whole calculation on the screen where other calculators show only the result of any calculation.

## Developing a 'feel' for numbers

Where number experiences involve a variety of situations and contexts, children will begin to develop a 'feel' for numbers that will be the foundation for calculating strategies and for using numbers effectively for problem-solving. Consider, for example, the numbers 16 and 17. Although very close in size, 16 has a 'nice feel' about it being 'double 8' or '4 × 4', while 17 has fewer convenient relationships with other numbers. The 'double' numbers, which appear to be the easiest to remember as number bonds, all appear in the sequence of counting in 2s. These numbers are also called 'even' numbers while all the others which are not multiples of two are called 'odd'. There is no easy way to remember these names, although the visual image of an odd number of items can always involve an arrangement of pairs with one 'odd' item that cannot be paired. Since the mathematical meaning of these words, odd and even, are different from their meanings in ordinary English, some discussion will be necessary to establish the conventions that will be assumed when working with these numbers.

Although the name 'even' is given to all multiples of two, there are no particular names for multiples of three, four, five, etc. There are, however, characteristics that such numbers possess that can become familiar to children when the number symbols are used. Counting in fives gives only the numbers ending in 5 or 0, while counting in fours will give only even numbers. Counting in threes, '3, 6, 9, 12, 15, 18, 21, 24, 27, 30 ...', will give numbers that are alternately odd and even and whose digits always add up to 3 or 6 or 9. Such 'discoveries' can be fascinating and attempts to explain the reasons behind these findings will help reinforce the logical nature of the number system and the patterns within it.

There will be some numbers that rarely appear in patterns because they are not multiples of any other number. Numbers such as 13, 17 and 31 are multiples only of themselves and one, and are called 'prime' numbers. What is fascinating about the prime numbers is the fact that they do not appear regularly in the counting sequence and there is no easy way to 'test' a number to see if a number is prime, apart from trying all of the possible factors it could have. Other characterizations of numbers can include 'square', 'triangular' and 'cube' numbers that are so named because of the way they can be made with geometric arrangements (Figure 3.5).

There are many relationships that can be explored and some interesting patterns that emerge as these numbers are constructed in different ways, for example the way adding consecutive odd numbers gives a total that is a square number:

$$1 = 1$$
$$4 = 1 + 3$$
$$9 = 1 + 3 + 5$$
$$16 = 1 + 3 + 5 + 7$$

Although numbers have a utilitarian nature for representing and solving problems, the number system has a beauty in the logical relationships that exist and the patterns that can be generated. Developing children's fascination for numbers will encourage not only 'number sense' but also an ability to observe and analyse relationships involving skills that will have applications throughout and beyond mathematics.

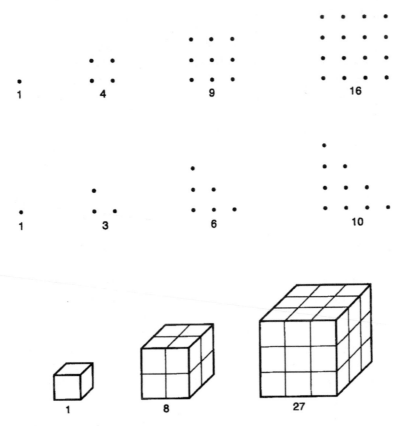

**Figure 3.5** 'Square', 'triangular' and 'cube' numbers.

## Activities

1.  When you next walk around a supermarket, look at all the numbers and the way they are displayed. Make a collection of printed numbers that are used in interesting or familiar contexts, for example, supermarket checkout tickets, cinema tickets or food wrappers.
2.  Look at the way numerals are shown on a calculator and draw these representations on paper. Find the largest number that can be displayed. See what happens when you add 11 more.

# CHAPTER 4

# Addition and Subtraction

The operations of addition and subtraction can be introduced through experiences relating to combining and partitioning collections of objects. Ideas of these operations begin to be formalized when the results are expressed using particular language, and later symbolic format. There are other operations on numbers that are not so readily formalized, for example halving and doubling, and it is important to remember that addition and subtraction form only part of a child's experiences with numbers. Rearranging collections can give a feel for numbers if there is discussion to accompany the activity, for example, 6 is 3 and 3, or 2 and 2 and 2, or 2 more than 4. In the early stages of learning about arithmetic operations, informal ideas are developed so that children are confident working orally and with diagrammatic representations before any symbols are introduced. With careful progression the symbols will provide a shorthand way to record results that children already know, but premature introduction will cause difficulties.

The very words 'addition' and 'subtraction' make it clear that these arithmetic operations are a classroom formalization of certain processes that are associated with numbers. These words are rarely used outside school and many children will take time to associate them with their existing knowledge in the same way that it takes time to acquire new words and phrases in language. The terms themselves bring together a wealth of meanings that can be associated with the symbols '+' and '−'. Words such as 'add', 'plus', 'together make', 'take away', 'minus', 'subtract' and 'difference between' gives some indication of the diversity of language that needs to be mastered in children's developing understanding of context and situations that will later be symbolized.

## Formalizing language

There are many stages in building links between new words, existing experiences, and the knowledge of numbers that children already possess. In the first stages, children will begin to acquire informal understanding of addition and subtraction, both inside and outside the classroom, by observing patterns as they arrange and rearrange collections. This will involve manipulation of real materials that children will later visualize, and it is important that children begin to talk about numbers so that they appreciate connections with their existing knowledge. In discussion, children and teachers can talk about the way numbers relate to different situations and introduce words such as 'altogether', 'makes', 'take away' and 'leaves', and expressions such as 'one more, two more ... ten more' and 'one less, two less ... ten less'. In these early stages the focus should be on the number relationships that are generated, as much as the actions involved, since number sense develops as children become aware of the consistency in some of their findings.

They will come to know that '4 and 2 more' always results in 6, and that '4 and 3 more' is 7, one more than 6. Already there are connections to be made, as their 'bank' of known facts and strategies for deriving new facts is developed. Before any recording takes place the next stage involves refining the language for addition and subtraction with expressions like '4 and 2 more' replaced by '4 add 2', and '4 take away 2' replaced by '4 subtract 2'. At this stage it is important to use a whole variety of language so that addition is about 'increasing' and 'more than', and subtraction includes 'difference between'. For example, two measures may be compared using a subtraction calculation: 'If a toy truck is balanced by 8 cubes and a car is balanced by 5 cubes, what is the difference in their weights?' relates to 8 subtract 5.

## Relating addition and subtraction to counting

The practical activity of adding one more to a collection or taking one away will provide additional language and experiences with counting which will help children to associate the concrete models with some abstract number patterns. When the practical idea of 'one more' is associated with the next number in a counting sequence, and 'one less' is associated with the previous number, these patterns can begin to be identified with 'add one' and 'subtract one'.

This is initially achieved through problems that have meaning for the children like adding a bead to a necklace, sorting coloured counters for a game, or organizing the children themselves into groups. Many of the more contrived activities with classroom materials, like colouring pictures on a worksheet, leave children confused about the activity's purpose and provide little motivation for finding answers. When children are happy to respond verbally to questions about 'one more/add one' and 'one less/subtract one', representations including arrows, 'function machines' for changing numbers, and 'hops on the number line' may be introduced to record some findings (Figure 4.1). It is also worth noting that none of the representations in Figure 4.1 involve the 'equals' symbol, which needs careful introduction if its true meaning is to be used and it is not restricted to the interpretation of 'makes'.

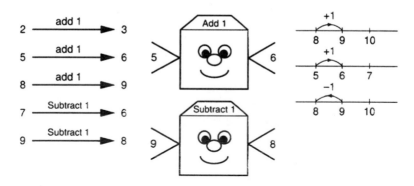

**Figure 4.1** Recording 'one more' and 'one less' with 'arrows', 'function machines' and 'hops' on the number line.

Although it may be tempting to read the symbols '− 1' as 'take away one', this will limit the circumstances in which the symbol can be used and give a false impression of the meaning that will have to be re-learned later. The word 'minus' is also used but the association of 'add' with addition and 'subtract' with subtraction may be helpful. Numbers need not be limited in the activity of 'adding one'. As soon as children can count beyond twenty, larger numbers can be used to focus on the changes that take place as each 'decade number' is reached. For example, '16 add 1', '19 add 1' or '39 add 1' can be associated with addition and, at the same time, used to reinforce the vocabulary of counting. 'Subtract 1' may be similarly associated with counting backwards. Examples such as '20 subtract 1' can be used to assess children's understanding of the way the number system is constructed.

## Practical problems

There is research evidence to show that very young pupils can find solutions to calculations even if they lack sophisticated mathematical techniques, suggesting that the mathematics is developed out of problem-solving rather than learned separately and then applied (Hughes, 1986; Beishuizen, 1995). Real activities such as keeping the score in a bean bag catching game (or real questions such as 'How many in red team if one more comes in?') will motivate children to find answers to numerical problems. Dates on a calendar provide a familiar context for larger numbers (for example, 'Today is the 19th. What will be the date tomorrow?'). Games, songs and stories can also be used to breach the reality/abstraction divide and will introduce variety into situations that can involve numbers. For example, rhymes such as 'Ten fat sausages sizzling in a pan' or 'Ten green bottles' can be acted out or modelled with finger actions.

## Progressing to 'add 2'

The idea of 'add 2' is the next stage in this development and is associated with both the practical activity of adding two more objects to a set and also the more abstract notion of a number 'two further on' in the counting sequence. Practical activities of 'adding 2 more' can involve children in predicting the total, thereby helping establish the link with counting. Initially the count will be verbalized, but children can then be encouraged to count in a whisper and eventually 'count in your head'. Small numbers may relate to familiar number facts such as '4 and 2 more is 6' but larger numbers such as '20 and 2 more' or '29 and 2 more' will again help to establish relationships with the structure of the number system. This approach is different from the more usual introduction to addition where two small collections are put together and counted. It helps to establish the relationship between adding and counting and uses the idea that one of the numbers is used as the starting point for a counting procedure.

## Progression in counting strategies for addition

In the more traditional introduction to addition involving the combining of two sets of objects, there is progression evident in the procedures children use for finding the total number of objects. These procedures are identified by Carpenter and Moser (1983) in their analysis of children's addition and subtraction strategies. There are a number of stages that have been identified in procedures for finding the answer to '3 add 5'. In the first stage, a set of 3 objects (or fingers) is combined with a set of 5 objects (or fingers) and the sets are put together and all objects are counted '1, 2, 3 ... 4, 5, 6, 7, 8' in a strategy termed *counting all*. At the next stage the inefficiency is recognized as children realize that it is not necessary to re-count the first set. The collection is now counted '3 ... 4, 5, 6, 7, 8' in a procedure termed *counting on*. This counting is more complex than the first stage since many young children are able to count more successfully when they start at one than when they start at any other number. It is also complicated by the need to maintain a double count ('4, 5, 6, 7, 8' identified with '1 more, 2 more ... 5 more') and some action may be needed so that physical movements support the count. It is at this stage that a misconception can occur when the first number uttered (the count for the first set) becomes confused with the numbers to be added. This can also be seen where children point to numbers on a number line and count the number symbols they touch instead of the spaces they move across. If this misconception is formed it may be necessary to encourage children to use materials and the 'count all' strategy as a check.

A further development in strategy occurs with the recognition that '3 add 5' gives the same total as '5 add 3', this is known as the *commutative law for addition*, and Carpenter and Moser (1983) described this next stage as *counting on from the larger*. When this relationship is recognized the count may be shortened to '5 ... 6, 7, *8*', sometimes supported by the imagined action of first 'putting the 5 in your head'. Children may be better motivated to use such a shortcut when larger numbers are introduced such as '2 add 15' and '3 add 49'. There is evidence that children progress through these stages of 'counting all', 'counting on' and 'counting on from the larger number' before they come to recognize that '3 and 5 together *always* make 8' – a *number fact*. It is by focusing on the number relationships that are generated, as well as the procedures for generating them, that children are helped in developing number sense.

Complications with addition may arise where the number zero is involved. The sum $5 + 0 = ?$ is often interpreted as '5 add nothing' – therein lies an immediate difficulty – if there is nothing to add then what can the question be requiring? Teachers may give a context, for example, '5 cats are sitting on a wall and no more cats come along so how many cats are on the wall?' Too frequently this is seen by children as a ritualistic game with little purpose. Equally difficult can be subtractions like $5 - 5 = ?$ where the answer is zero. Problem like these, together with $5 - 0 = ?$, and later $5 \times 0 = ?$, have important consequences when calculations with double digit numbers like 20 or 102 are involved. Teachers suggesting contexts may provide a short-term solution to the difficulty but, in general, it is only clear that children have understanding where they are able to provide their own context for such problems.

Observing children as they calculate will help identify the stage of development of each individual although this is not easy with a large class of children. Children who rely on counting the actual objects can be encouraged to visualize the situation by using a cover over the objects or working with their eyes shut to *think about* the objects involved. The next level of abstraction involves the objects being replaced by fingers to be counted, or by actions like finger tapping or nods of the head. Until the stage of working with abstract number facts is achieved, children will be hampered in their progress to more complex calculations.

## Number facts

Among the many number facts that are established through practical activities, some will be particularly important in forming the basis upon which further arithmetic is built. Rapid recall of the number pairs that make ten (called *number bonds to ten* or *complements in ten*) will be crucial for later calculations and these form important 'benchmarks' that children will refer to constantly. In the initial stages of calculating, confident recall of these number facts will be more important than any formal recording. Different resources will be helpful in providing visual imagery to support the association of number pairs. A bead string with ten beads in two colours (see Chapter 1) can be given to each child who can then rearrange the beads to show different number pairs. Arranging the beads into two lots of five makes number recognition easier (for example, 6 is seen as 5 and 1 more) and may be associated with the fingers on each hand (Figure 4.2).

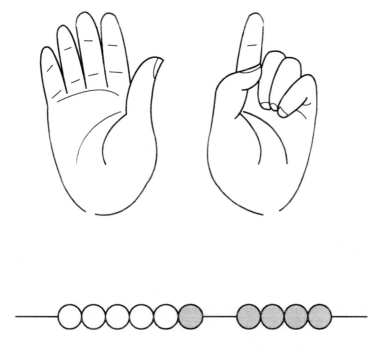

**Figure 4.2**   6 is 5 and 1 more.

Children are also able to relate the facts they know to new calculations and when they can add 2 and 3, they have the potential to relate this knowledge to '*two* hundred add *three* hundred'. Young children revel in the experiences of working with very large numbers and these applications help them to understand that mathematics involves a pattern of related ideas. Because of the language we use, extension is not so clear for the decade numbers and written recording may help to extend the pattern to '20 add 30'.

Adding to the decade numbers is also important for instant recall, for example, '40 add 3' or '100 add 3' and it is notable that these are easy to verbalize but more difficult to record. When the children are secure with oral work discussion can be introduced of how the resulting numbers can be recorded.

## Progression in counting strategies for subtraction

For subtraction, Carpenter and Moser (1983) note a progression in stages similar to those they identify for addition. These are illustrated for finding $9 - 3$:

- 'count out' where the child may count out 9 fingers, lower 3, and count those remaining;
- 'counting back *from*', where the child counts from the larger number, 9, as many counted number words as the smaller number: '9 ... 8, 7, *6*';
- 'counting down *to*' where the backward count goes from the higher number down to the smaller number: '9 ... 8, 7, 6, 5, 4, 3', tallying to get the answer *6*;
- 'count *up*' from 3 to 9; and
- 'using known facts and derived facts'.

These different approaches are sometimes evident in children's finger methods, for example in the calculations '9 – 2' and '9 – 7', where the most effective strategies would be 'counting down from 9' (9 ... 8, *7*) and 'counting down to 7' (9 ... 8, 7) respectively. Although the words and actions may be exactly the same in these two finger methods (try them for yourself!) the solutions relate, in the first case, to the *last number spoken*, '7', and in the second to the *number of words uttered* between 9 and 7. It is easy to underestimate the understanding shown, and even the children themselves may not realize the different methods they are using. Watching children will help teachers assess the strategies they are using. Sharing discussion of their explanations will give children opportunities to broaden their own range of calculating strategies.

At this stage, developing number sense involves *meta-cognition* as children reflect on some of the answers to problems and find connections. Some children will realize for themselves that $9 - 7$ may equally well be solved using an addition strategy (counting from 7 to 9) but others will need this idea to be pointed out explicitly, and they will need to see the ways addition and subtraction relate in practical situations. It is not only the numbers 9, 7 and 2 that are related but the operations themselves that are 'inverse operations', operations that work in reverse, and involve precisely the same number triple. The connection between addition and subtraction as 'inverse operations' can be explored using diagrams (Figure 4.3), and the empty number line, explained in more detail in the next chapter, provides a good illustration.

When using number diagrams such as that shown in Figure 4.3, depending on which number or operation boxes are left blank, the problem can focus on links that can be made. Blank diagrams may be filled in by the children who will also find it challenging to construct similar problems for each other.

## Relating addition and subtraction

Associated with every addition fact are two subtraction facts that are immediately available without the need for any calculation. If '5 and 3 together make 8' this also means that '8 is 3 more than 5' and '8 is 5 more than 3', or that '8 subtract 3 is 5' and '8 subtract 5 is 3'. Before isolating addition and subtraction in written recording, work can be done to identify *number triples* and explore different ways to record the findings diagrammatically and with numbers.

| 3 | 5 |
|---|---|
| 8 ||

Many children who achieve early success in addition and subtraction do so by recognizing that what is required is the third

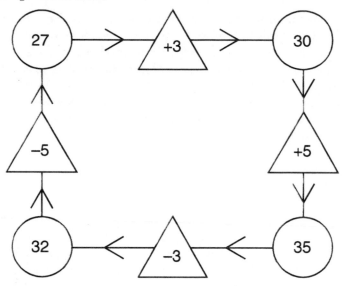

**Figure 4.3**  Diagram to show + and − as inverse operations.

number in such a number triple. This remains a powerful strategy and marks early differences between children who 'just know the answer' and those who continue to count. To develop number sense teachers will need to make explicit reference to the way number triples can be used and the way new facts can be derived from those that are already known. The easiest facts for children to remember appear to be the 'doubles' ('2 add 2', '3 add 3', '4 add 4', etc.) and other numbers can be associated as 'near doubles'. For example, '5 add 6' can be identified as one more than 10, or '8 add 7' as one more than 14. Making this kind of link not only helps children to derive new facts from the ones they already know, but also helps to establish strategies for calculating. Rather than using a counting strategy, children should be encouraged to link new questions to any facts that they already know. Discussion of all the various approaches they suggest will help children become flexible in their approaches to problem-solving and it can be fruitful to spend some time considering different approaches to a single problem rather than tackling several problems that are not connected.

## Transforming problems and making connections

A powerful strategy for calculating is to transform the problem and use an easier procedure (or easier numbers) than those that are given. When children learn that $9 - 4$ can be solved by *adding* an appropriate number to 4, they can either use a counting-on strategy, or a number fact $(4 + 5 = 9)$ to solve the problem. It is possible not only to change the procedure from subtraction to addition but also to change the numbers using a system of *compensation*. Knowing that $10 - 4$ results in 6, it may be immediately clear that $9 - 4$ gives one less. Underlying all calculations are the basic facts and, most importantly, the connections that children continue to establish about the way numbers relate to each other. Gray and Tall (1994) extend their idea of a precept to explain why children of differing abilities with apparently the same knowledge of number facts solve addition and subtraction problems in different ways (see Chapter 3). To add $5 + 9$ can be a challenging task if you do not have the precept that 9 is $10 - 1$ (which in turn relates to the idea that 9 is the counting number before 10). They suggest the phrase 'slow learner' is a misnomer because the less able do not simply learn the same techniques more slowly, they develop different techniques. Even the process of reversing addition to give subtraction is seen by the less successful child as a new process (counting back instead of counting up). The proceptual thinker is faced with a far easier task as counting, addition and subtraction are all operating with the same number precept, which allows numbers to be decomposed or reconstructed and used in related procedures for calculation purposes.

## Recording addition and subtraction facts

When working with schemes or texts, addition and subtraction are sometimes introduced pictorially or diagrammatically with rapid progress to the symbols which are explained by the teacher. With repeated practice of particular procedures, many children may come to understand these operations as a particular 'ritual' that they do not associate with their wider experiences with numbers. In writing about current practices in the early-years classroom, Aubrey (1997) expresses concern that 'scheme work *determined* when and how addition and subtraction were introduced'. Working from schemes, teachers work as mediators between their pupils and the text, and although children may learn how to do 'sums' in this way, the justification for particular methods of recording and the meanings of all the symbols are not made explicit.

The reason that the relationship between numbers such as 5, 3 and 8 is recorded as $5 + 3 = 8$ is not always clear to children. This result could equally well be written as $(5, 3) + = 8$ and read as '5 and 3 added together make 8'. This corresponds to the actions 'make a collection of 5 and a collection of 3 and put them together'. The answer relates to a particular convention, just as there is a convention about the way to spell a word like 'boat'. This is not the only possible way to record this result and it could equally well be symbolized as $8 = 5 + 3$ and read 'we found 8 when we added 5 and 3'. Difficulty with the 'equals' sign will arise if it is always seen to precede the answer and is interpreted as 'makes'. Early recording needs to involve a variety of formats to show how symbols can be used and interpreted in a variety of ways.

If children are to focus on the numerical results, flexibility in recording will need be introduced from the earliest stages and patterns in the numerical results made the focus of attention:

$$8 = 5 + 3$$
$$8 = 6 + 2$$
$$8 = 7 + 1$$
$$8 = 8 + 0$$

Another purpose for recording will be to establish patterns that will enable children to derive new results from those that are already known (Figure 4.4). An attractive wall display can be made where children share and compare their findings while all working at their own level.

## Reading the symbols

Symbolic representation will be used to ask questions as well as for recording findings. This may help to establish links between a

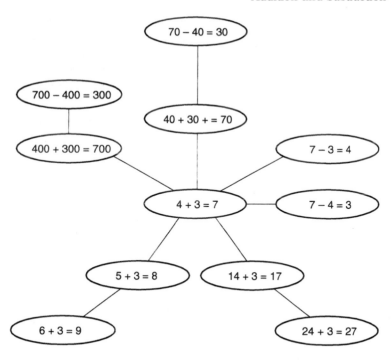

**Figure 4.4** A web of results derived from 4 + 3 = 7.

variety of questions involving the same number triple. Children will need to use and understand some complex mathematical language when 'reading' or 'putting into words' the relationships in 'missing number' problems as such problems can help to establish that symbols can be interpreted in flexible ways. Consider the following examples:

| | | |
|---|---|---|
| 3 + □ = 8 | □ + 3 = 8 | 3 = 8 − □ |
| 5 = □ − 3 | □ − 5 = 3 | 8 = 5 + □ |

In attempting to 'read' the symbols, some expressions will be more difficult to verbalize than others. The expression '8 − □' may be related to a set of 8 objects from which some are removed, while '□ − 3' represents a situation which may be referred to as 'start unknown'. Those who understand the relationship between 3, 8 and 5 may *know* the answer, otherwise a 'trial and improve' strategy may be used for children who are stuck. A question such as 'Could it be 4?' will sometimes help individuals to work from some of the facts that they already know. 'Will the number be bigger than 4 or smaller than 4?' will not only help lead to a solution but will also provide a strategy of trying other numbers and making deductions from these findings – an important strategy in developing number sense. In such problems, the learning objective for children will be to establish ways of 'reading' the expressions and relating them to procedures. Teachers will need to be thoughtful in the ways they give support to those in difficulty without 'giving' them interpretations for these problems.

Problems presented in word form generate difficulties of a different kind. When all the words are given, the task becomes one of interpreting the meaning of the question and identifying it with an addition or subtraction procedure. Word problems will vary in their semantic structure and Dickson *et al.* (1984) identify different types of word problem that can be represented as $3 + 2 = 5$. They include such word problems as 'John has 3 large cars and 2 small cars. How many cars does he have altogether?' which they identify as the *union* aspect of addition. Alternatively, 'John has 3 cars. Jane has 2 more cars than John. How many cars does Jane have?' which is referred to as the *comparison* aspect of addition. Children's strategies for solving these two problems would probably be quite different with the second presenting more difficulty than the first.

Carpenter and Moser (1983) give one of the most complete analyses of addition and subtraction word problems distinguishing classes of problems on the basis of their semantic structure. They identified four main types of problem: *change, combine, compare* and *equalize*, each with subclasses of addition and subtraction problems. They show that children's solution processes clearly reflect the structure of the problem as well as the numbers involved, with some presenting much more difficulty than others.

The active, 'change' problems involve a procedure within the problem, contrasts with the passive, 'combine' problems which

**Table 4.1**   Four main types of addition and subtraction word problems

| change | Mara has 5 marbles. Ben gives her 8 more marbles. How many does she have altogether? | Ben has 8 marbles and he gives 3 to Mara. How many does he have left? |
|---|---|---|
| combine/ separate | Mara has 5 blue marbles and 8 red marbles. How many marbles does she have? | Together Ben and Mara have 13 marbles. If Ben has 5, how many does Mara have? |
| compare | Mara has 8 marbles and Ben has 5 marbles. How many more than Mara does Ben have? | Ben has 5 marbles. He has 8 fewer than Mara. How many does Mara have? |
| equalize | Mara has 8 marbles and Ben has 5 marbles. How many must Ben find to have the same as Mara? | Mara has 5 marbles. If Ben loses 8 marbles he will have the same number as Mara. How many does Ben have? |

suggest no procedure. Although the difference may appear to be subtle, the image of further marbles being 'given' suggests actions that could be used to find the result of the first problem, whereas the second has no such actions. Contrast these with the 'compare' problem: 'Mara has 5 marbles. Ben has 8 more that Mara. How many marbles does Ben have?' This third problem is more difficult because the imagery it presents is much more complex and a third subset of marbles, or a complete set including all of Ben's, needs to be visualized. Although all of these problems can be symbolized by the expression '8 + 5 = 13', they relate to different representations including all the different missing-numbers problems. For example, $\square - 8 = 5$ may be related to 'Ben has 5 marbles. He has 8 fewer than Mara. How many does Mara have?' Each will present differing levels of difficulty for children.

Teachers can help to develop their pupils' understanding by introducing a wide range of semantic structures and making these the basis for discussion. Although it is tempting to simplify the wording of a problem, or to give an alternative interpretation to children in order that the calculation can be attempted, this is a situation in which much of the mathematical learning relates to the words and meanings, rather than the arithmetic calculations. Children themselves should gain experience by making up word problems to match addition and subtraction calculations, and groups can work together to give a number of alternatives for any number problems they are given.

## Working mentally with larger numbers

Counting on and counting back will help establish answers to various problems but this counting needs to be made more efficient by introducing 'chunks' that relate counting to established number facts. Adding 7 and 3 to make 10, for example, should become an established 'benchmark' fact so that any number 'ending' in 7 is associated with the 'chunk' 3. Working with an 'empty number line' can help give a visual image that encourages progression from 'hops' that represent 'counting in ones' to 'jumps' using different 'chunks' that illustrate such known facts (Figure 4.5).

**Figure 4.5** 17 + 3 using a jump of 3 on the empty number line.

Using known facts will provide an efficient strategy for working 'within decade boundaries' but may not be quite so easily related to calculations that go 'across decade boundaries'.

| within decade boundaries | 12 + 3 = <br> 25 + 4 = <br> 84 + 3 = |
|---|---|
| across decade boundaries | 17 + 5 = <br> 25 + 6 = <br> 84 + 8 = |

It will be possible to use the 'benchmark' facts involving the number bonds for ten for the latter of these types of problem using a strategy sometimes referred to as 'bridging to ten'. This involves partitioning the number to be added so that the first 'chunk' takes the total to a decade number and then the remaining units are added.

| Adding by 'bridging to ten' | 17 + 5 = <br> 25 + 6 = <br> 84 + 8 = | 17 + 3 + 2 = 20 + 2 <br> 25 + 5 + 1 = 30 + 1 <br> 84 + 6 + 2 = 90 + 2 |
| --- | --- | --- |

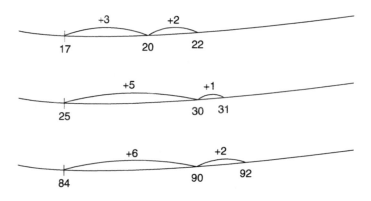

**Figure 4.6** 'Bridging to tens' on an empty number line.

Another 'benchmark' in children's understanding relates to their understanding of the effect of starting at any number and adding ten. This should be automatic for children before two-digit addition and subtraction are introduced and those who do not *know* that 24 add 10 gives 34 will need to spend more time with calculators, bead strings or 'tens' and 'units' structured apparatus to establish these patterns of results. For certain calculations, particularly those involving numbers that end in 1 or 2, and 8 or 9, an easier calculation is possible by changing the calculation using a procedure sometimes referred to as *compensating*. Adding 28, for example, can be achieved by adding 30 and subtracting 2 from the result. In Chapter 5, addition and subtraction will be related to counting using the image of an empty number line which can be used to support the different mental strategies that children will learn.

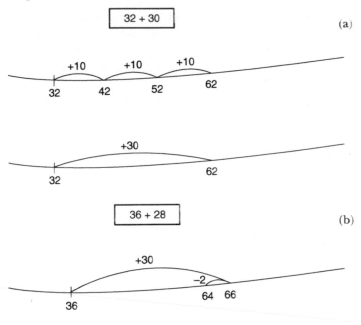

**Figure 4.7**   (a)  Empty number lines with three jumps of 10 and one jump of 30.
(b)  Adding 28 by going forward 30 and back 2.

## Mental methods for adding and subtracting two two-digit numbers

Mental strategies for adding or subtracting two two-digit numbers fall into two main categories, *sequence methods* and *split tens methods*, according to whether they are related to 'counting' or to 'place value'. *Sequence methods* retain one number as a whole and partition the other into convenient 'chunks' to add or subtract. *Split tens methods* partition both numbers into tens and units. Some of the different ways to 'think about' the addition calculation 27 + 35 can be represented in the following ways:

| Sequence methods | Split tens methods |
|---|---|
| 27 + 35 = (27 + 30) + 5 | 27 + 35 = (20 + 30) + (7 + 5) |
| 27 + 35 = (27 + 3) + 2 + 30 | 27 + 35 = (7 + 5) + (20 + 30) |
| 27 + 35 = (20 + 35) + 7 | |
| 27 + 35 = (35 + 5) + 22 | Compensation method |
| | 27 + 35 = (25 + 2) + (25 + 10) = 50 + 12 |

It is notable that mental split tens methods retain the wholeness of the numbers so that a number such as 27 may be regarded as '20 and 7' rather that '2 tens and 7 units'. The latter is introduced in the very curtailed written algorithms that will be discussed in Chapter 6.

These same approaches may form the basis for subtraction strategies. Some of the different ways to 'think about' the subtraction calculation 45 − 27 can be represented in the following ways:

| Sequence methods | Split tens methods |
|---|---|
| 45 − 27 = (45 − 20) − 7 = 25 − 7 | 45 − 27 = (40 + 5) − (20 + 7) = (30 + 15) − (20 + 7) = (30 − 20) + (15 − 7) |
| 45 − 27 = (45 − 5) − 20 − 2 = 40 − 20 − 2 | 45 − 27 = (40 + 5) − (20 + 7) = (40 + 15) − (30 + 7) = (40 − 30) + (15 − 7) this method, known as 'equal additions', used to be the most commonly taught algorithm |
| 45 − 27 = (47 − 27) − 2 a 'transformation' method | |

This subtraction calculation can also be effectively related to addition and undertaken by 'counting on' from 27 to 45 and all the experiences of addition methods can be used in mental methods for subtraction. An efficient example is the following:

From 27 to 47 is 20, so from 27 to 45 is 2 less, that is 18

Fuson *et al.* (1997) suggest a similar classification of strategies in their references to three classes of methods used for addition and subtraction of two-digit numbers. They identify these methods for the calculations 38 + 26:

- *sequence methods* such as counting on by tens and ones, for example, begin with one number and move up or down the sequence by tens or ones, e.g. 38, 48, 58, 59, 60, 61, 62, 63, 64;
- *collected multiunit methods* in which the tens and then the ones are counted or added, for example, 30 and 20 is 50; 8 and 6 is 14, now add 50 and 14 to get the answer 64; and
- *concatenated single digits* in which the numbers are used as strings of digits, for example, 8 and 6 is 14, which gives four units and one ten to 'carry', 3 and 2 is 5 with the one carried forward makes 6 to get 6 ... 4 as the answer.

This last method is usually associated with a vertical layout where the children add or subtract separate columns. Whereas the first two methods deal at all stages with the whole numbers, retaining their values, the third deals with the digits only and it is the positioning in a written calculation that gives them their value. These methods are not always used separately but may be mixed, for example, with tens added or subtracted and then a sequence method used to add or subtract the remaining ones. For example, to calculate 38 + 26 as combination of 'chunking' and counting in ones: 30 and 20 is 50, 50 and 8 is 58, 59, 60, 61, 62, 63, 64.

Fuson also identifies the 'transformation' method in which both numbers are changed to make an easier calculation. For example, 38 and 26 gives the same total as 40 add 24.

Thompson (1997) uses different category names but identifies broadly the same categories in his analysis of the mental strategy used by children:

- *cumulative sum* starts with one number (most efficiently the largest one), increases this number by the appropriate multiple of ten and then adds the units either by counting on or by using complements in 10 – 38, 48, 58 and 2 makes 60 and then 4 more make 64;
- *partial sums* works separately with the 'tens' and 'units'; and

- *cumulo-partial sums* – initially adding the tens and then using this new number as the start for a cumulative method.

Thompson suggests that children who are not taught formal written methods will develop their own, often idiosyncratic, methods and suggests different layouts for written recording that can 'match' the child's individual approach. These will be discussed in a later chapter.

## Analysing errors

Ginsburg (1977) suggests that mistakes associated with written methods are often based on rules that have been misapplied, for example always subtracting the smaller digit from the larger in subtraction. These are more likely to occur where children are trying to follow rules they have learned without adequate understanding. Where procedures for calculating have been 'given' to children they can see arithmetic as an arbitrary game of following rules with the answers depending on the rules you follow. Teachers sometimes worry about allowing children to discuss their own approaches to a problem in case wrong ideas are suggested. Their inclination is always to ask children who are likely to be correct to explain their methods. Research, on the other hand, shows that learning is more effective when common misconceptions are exposed, addressed and discussed in teaching (Askew and Wiliam, 1995, pp. 12–13). Drawing attention to a misconception before giving the examples is less effective than letting the pupils fall into the 'trap' and then having the discussion. It seems that to teach in a way that avoids creating *any* misconceptions (sometimes called 'faultless communication') is not possible and many misconceptions will remain hidden unless the teacher makes specific efforts to uncover them. Addressing misconceptions during teaching does actually improve achievement and long-term retention of mathematical skills and concepts.

## Activities

1. Identify some real-life situations that involve early ideas of addition and subtraction, such as working out how many

      people will be in the room if one or two arrive, or one or two leave.

2. Find a classroom resource that will illustrate the idea that addition and subtraction are inverse operations.

# CHAPTER 5

# The Empty Number Line

In the last chapter important ideas for the operations of addition and subtraction began to grow out of counting skills. Some 'sequence' methods were introduced for mental calculating involving whole numbers, as an alternative to 'splitting' numbers into tens and units. These sequence methods relate well to the counting skills that children are learning and can be developed as mental strategies. In this chapter the 'empty number line' (that is a line with no markings at all) will be introduced to encourage written illustrations for supporting mental calculations, and later, to produce effective pencil and paper methods.

The empty number line was developed in the Netherlands as part of Realistic Mathematics Education (RME) and reflects developments that are receiving world wide acknowledgement for new approaches based on well-researched methods (van den Heuvel-Panhuizen, 2001). The RME approach aims to develop mathematics in a way that is meaningful to children by identifying a 'learning trajectory' that takes them from concrete situations to more abstract mathematics through a process of 'progressive mathematization' (Buys, 2001). Through a number of stages children learn mental strategies that will underpin more formal written methods, and they develop flexibility in tackling problems involving different numbers. The essence of this approach is the progressive development of efficiency without loss of understanding.

Starting with counting as a basic skill, children learn to associate counting up to 20 with images of beads arranged on a frame in groups of five. This imagery is later developed so that counting up to 100 is associated with beads arranged in tens on a bead string. The number line is progressively introduced, first with calibrations to match the counting words, then with only the decade numbers identified so that children learn to imagine where the intervening numbers must be placed, and finally with no markings except those determined by an individual. In this way, number relations are learned by associating them with different forms of counting and their associated images on the number line in a progression that will be outlined in this chapter.

A numbered line has been a useful resource for many generations but some children have found it difficult to move beyond simply counting in ones to more efficient calculating. By initially removing all the numbers except decade numbers, children are encouraged to imagine the position of other numbers. The empty format will later allow each individual to mark their own numbers and jumps so that they are stimulated to use mental imagery rather than more passively reading off given numbers.

The empty number line first appears widely in England in the *Framework for Teaching Mathematics* where it is used to illustrate informal methods for addition and subtraction in Year 3 (DfEE, 1999, pp. 67, 69). Teachers who follow the *Framework* will note that in these curriculum guidelines there is no preliminary preparation in Year 1 or Year 2 for this approach, and the following paragraphs will show that there are specific skills that need to be established if the empty number line is to be a meaningful model for calculating. As an innovation that enables individuals to model a mental strategy with their own pictorial record, a 'self-drawn' empty number line is identified in several government reports as an informal and effective method for calculating (Figure 5.1).

> The approach [to calculation] in the primary school builds on the use of the number line, first with numbers marked and then a blank line, to record steps in a calculation such as 47 + 26 ...
>
> (DfEE, 2001, p. 10)

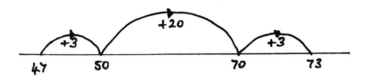

**Figure 5.1** Pupils make jottings to assist their mental calculations, e.g. 47 + 26.

## Empty number line as a model for counting

As seen in the last chapter, counting forward in ones, twos, tens or any other numbers may be associated with addition, and counting backwards associated with subtraction. The oral and mental starters to numeracy lessons provide good opportunities for children to become confident with counting in many different ways. These early ideas of counting forwards and backwards can be illustrated by movement along a bead string or on a bead frame when young children are working only orally, and later, when they begin recognizing symbols, on the number line. This helps children progressively build up an image to match the number words and the operations. This imagery starts with the counting sequence of words matched with groups of beads in different colours and it is helpful if this starts with each lot of ten beads grouped as two lots of five. The way the beads are grouped presents a powerful image that will help children to become aware of the way numbers relate to each other, for example, that four and one more makes five, or that five is made up of two and three.

## Progressive development from use of fingers and hands

Fingers are a wonderful resource for counting but impose limits when the numbers get bigger. A bead string of ten beads with five of each colour can provide a good first step away from fingers to a more adaptable resource. As soon as numbers become meaningful, each of the numbers from 1 to 10 can be seen on a bead frame or on a bead string, and a connection made between the cardinal and ordinal aspect of numbers (see Chapter 2). A bead frame of twenty beads (Chapter 1, Figure 1.1b) gives children imagery for the numbers up to 20 that will become more powerful than fingers.

Initially taking them from 1 to 10 and then to 20, the bead frame shows the structure of numbers, for example, 9 is the number just before 10, and 13 is 3 more than 10, relating these images to the counting they are familiar with. The important way that number names are based on grouping in tens begins to become clearer as a pattern is established for the number names beyond ten. As noted in Chapter 3, there can be difficulties with the names for numbers between 11 and 19, and it is important to combine verbal and visual activities with number representation through reading and writing with the symbols. Arranging the numbers along a line, at the same time as counting aloud, will give children their first number line, and can support counting forwards and backwards starting at any number.

The bead frame can also be used to illustrate important relations that will be the benchmarks for calculating, such as using doubles, for example, 6 is double 3, and 8 is double 4. This in turn can be used to find 'near doubles' such as 7 as double 3 and one more. A lot of discussion of the different ways numbers relate to each other can take place without moving beyond 20 as these relationships form the basis for much of the calculating that will come later. Investing time in developing children's understanding of these relationships and the way counting can be related to images of beads, and of a numbered line, will provide the foundation for mental calculation.

## The empty number line

Research has shown that images starting with the bead string can be modified progressively to a number line, and then an 'empty number line' to provide mental imagery for calculating strategies based on counting (Beishuizen, 1999). The 'empty number line' introduces the flexibility to take 'jumps' of any size in either direction and starting at any point, in a way that supports different mental strategies. Initially, movements one at a time can be associated with 'hops', and later 'jumps' can be associated with larger intervals (Menne, 2001). From having to count on 3 hops from 7 to 10, children will come to recognize that a single jump of 3 will cover the interval from 7 to 10 and this relates to the language that '7 and 3 more makes 10'. With such images, children can be encouraged to investigate and then predict the movements that are needed to get from one number to another. This is a crucial stage in understanding as it takes children beyond counting in ones to recognizing number facts. Working with a real bead string and then illustrating different calculations as jumps on a number line can begin in Key Stage 1, and will help with the transfer of understanding from concrete materials to a written representation.

There are several stages in learning to use an empty number

line and at each stage there are particular skills that need to be developed, such as *locating* numbers on the number line, identifying *jumps to a number* and *jumps from a number*, *bridging through ten* and making *jumps of ten*.

## Locating numbers on a number line

The first understanding children need to develop is where to place numbers in relation to each other. Initially working with numbers up to ten, children can be physically involved in pegging numbered cards in their appropriate place on a 'washing line'. (An alternative is to give individuals numbered cards and let them make a 'human washing line' by being arranged in the right order.) By associating this activity with counting they will begin to develop an image of the numbers in their order and the stability of the way they relate to each other. In time, as the children's counting skills develop, this locating of numbers can be extended to numbers up to 20 and up to 100. In the higher grades a 'washing line game' can involve very large numbers, negative numbers and fractions or decimals, as placing numbers like 0.1, 0.51, 0.05 and 0.15 in relation to each other will challenge children's understanding of this number representation.

## Moving from hops to jumps

As children become comfortable with the ordering of numbers they can begin to talk about their positions in relation to each other. To get from 5 to 7 will take '2 hops' or a 'jump of 2' and to get from 7 to 10 will take '3 hops' or a 'jump of 3' (Figure 5.2).

Counting backwards will help show that from 7 to 5 is going back 2 and from 10 to 7 is going back 3. This relates to an image of

**Figure 5.2** Hops and jumps on an empty number line.

addition as a jump to the right on a line and subtraction as the inverse with a jump to the left. (Although some children will be happy to arrange numbers in ascending or descending order along the line it is most helpful if they become consistent with the smaller numbers always to the left.)

## *Jumps to and from a number*

With their developing familiarity of counting, children can begin to predict what jump is needed to get, say, from 7 to 10, while still supporting this with counting silently if necessary. It is crucial at this stage that children memorize these jumps, which are called 'number bonds', as later calculating will involve larger numbers where counting is not an option. The number bonds for 10 can also be associated with the ways fingers can be arranged on two hands and this image will reinforce the number bonds for some children. In the Netherlands, teachers use the more emotive description of 'hearts in love' to describe the pairs that make ten, and illustrate this on heart-shaped cards (Menne, 2001). Without counting, children can be encouraged to see that ten is made out of '9 and 1', '8 and 2', '7 and 3' or '6 and 4' or 'double 5' and that these pairs of numbers can also be reversed. A game of matching cards with the number pairs that make ten is a good way to reinforce these facts as they are memorized. When children are familiar with larger numbers, these number bonds will be used to move in *jumps to* the nearest decade number, for example, from 7 to 10 can be associated with 17 to 20 and with 27 to 30 as each will require the same jump of 3. Telling a partner what numbers to add on a calculator, in order to get to a decade number from different starting numbers, makes a fun game of memorizing and using number bonds.

Children will also need to understand *jumps from* the decade numbers, such as, from 10 jump on 3 gets to 13, or from 40 jump on 7 gets to 47. These ideas will help with children's developing understanding of the number system and the way words and symbols are constructed. It may seem obvious to adults that 40 add 7 makes 47 but this is a pattern that needs to be learned and can cause a problem for some children.

*Bridging across ten*

It is difficult to see some jumps that go beyond the 10, such as the jump from 8 to 13, and these can be more easily identified by combining two jumps '8 to 10 and 10 to 13'. This is called 'bridging across ten' or 'bridging through ten' and is recognized in Qualification and Curriculum Authority reports as a 'good mental strategy' for calculating.

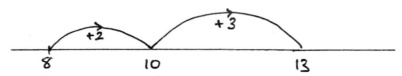

**Figure 5.3**  Bridging across 10 from 8 to 13.

This will be a useful strategy across all decade boundaries, 20, 30, 40 ..., for example, 28 add 6 can be achieved by jumping 2 to get to 30 and then jumping the remaining 4 to get to 34. This uses number bonds already learned and gives an image that relates to counting. Bridging across decade numbers is also a good way to manage subtraction, for example, 36 − 8 can be done mentally if it is broken into two steps, 36 − 6 and then 30 − 2, and an empty number line image will help to show why this works (Figure 5.4).

Such methods will encourage children to use number facts that they know rather than counting in ones. Later this idea will be

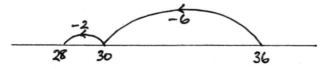

**Figure 5.4**  Subtraction by bridging across 30.

developed to bridging across the hundreds boundaries when a calculation such as 185 + 46 can be calculated as 185 + 15 + 31. Such working with larger numbers will be considered further in Chapter 7.

## *Jumps of ten*

A separate skill is knowing where you will 'land' after a jump of ten. Some children recognize quickly that starting at 24 and jumping forward ten will get you to 34, but others will take some time to learn this. Jumping backwards ten, for example from 57 back to 47, can be associated with counting backwards in tens from different starting points if this is a familiar activity. The illustration (Figure 5.5) shows a 'tens catcher' which has been developed to give images on the bead string of what happens when ten is added to or subtracted from any number (Menne, 2001).

**Figure 5.5** A 'tens catcher'.

These ideas can be explored and reinforced if a calculator is used to add 10, or subtract 10, from any two-digit number. This is a good use of the calculator to explore the important patterns you get when adding or subtracting 10, and can stimulate thinking if there is discussion of the patterns that appear and attempts at explanation. For a more challenging activity, 10 can be added to any three- or four-digit number, predicting the outcome before pressing the buttons, so that the effect can be identified with the different digit positions of the numbers. A game can be played in pairs where one child enters a chosen number on the calculator as the other has to predict the outcome when adding or subtracting 10. With numbers such as 998 to add 10, or 307 to subtract 10, this can make an interesting exploration with a calculator.

Once 10 can be added to any number, the empty number line can be used to record results and multiples of 10 can be introduced. Three 'jumps' of 10 can be replaced by the quicker 'jump' of 30 all in one go.

## *Clever calculating*

One major advantage of the empty number line as an aid to calculating is the ownership retained by each individual, as they identify where to put their numbers, and decide what hops and jumps to use. Children will work with the number facts that they know and can introduce more efficiency when they are confident. The calculation below, 185 + 48, can be broken down in many ways on the empty number line, such as adding 10 at a time to get 225, and then adding 5 and 3, or by adding 5 and then 10 followed by 33. An example of 'clever calculating' is the strategy of *compensating* where numbers are close to decade numbers. Adding 9 to a number, for example, can be achieved by adding 10 and subtracting 1. On the empty number line this is represented as 'a jump forward of 10 and a hop back of 1' and is associated with the learned skill of adding ten to a number. The calculation 185 + 48 could be done by jumping forward 50 to 235 (perhaps as 20 and 30), and back 2 to 233.

**Figure 5.6**   Compensating to calculate 185 + 48.

Similarly, subtracting 38 by 'subtracting 40 and adding 2' will be represented as a jump backwards of 40 and a jump forward of 2 to compensate for having subtracted too many. With many different options for calculating on the empty number line it becomes important for children to make decisions about which strategy to use. The operations of addition and subtraction no longer trigger an automatic response but the different numbers in a calculation should be taken into consideration and known number facts used wherever possible.

Each of the calculations 10 + 7, 19 + 7 and 23 + 7 may trigger a different known fact and a different mental method. Classroom discussions about which strategies are most effective will encourage flexibility in approaches to calculating and alert children to the importance of using number sense.

## Multiplication and division on the empty number line

By taking jumps of equal size on the empty number line an image of multiplication, and a pattern of related numbers, can be shown.

Children enjoy counting in twos or fives and tens, and the images of jumps will reinforce the number patterns that can be extended beyond 20 and up to 100. The written patterns will also help children to work beyond their memory, and reflect on the multiplication patterns that are produced. The multiples of 2, for example, will give all the even numbers, while multiples of 5 are all the numbers ending in 5 or 0. The patterns for threes or sevens are much more complex and will need a lot more experience before they can be memorized.

When these patterns of numbers become familiar, the question of 'how many jumps' are needed to get to a particular number will relate multiplication and division facts. As will be seen in the next chapter, multiplication and division are different ways of understanding the relationships that exist for a triple of numbers, for example 2, 3 and 6. Six is '2 lots of 3' or '3 lots of 2' identifies a relationship that can be expressed in a number of ways, and used to answer a range of questions. 'How many 2s are in 6?' and 'three 2s make 6' show the way division and multiplication can be related, and jumps on a number line will illustrate this connection. In preparation for division with remainders, it is a good idea to discuss the numbers around the multiples. The pattern of sixes, for example, includes the numbers 6, 12, 18, 24, 30, 36 and so on. With a number line showing these jumps, look at 23 and 25 which are both one hop away from 24. Describing these numbers and how they relate to the multiple of 6 introduces the important idea of 25 being 'four 6s and 1 more' while 23 is 'three 6s and 5 more'. Working with multiples on a number line and discussing *close* numbers will help children not only remember the multiples but also develop number sense for multiplication and division.

It is not a good idea to jump back from every number when doing division as unfamiliar patterns of numbers will not be helpful. Where a division is not exact, for example 'how many 2s in 19?' it is better to look for a *close* number that is a multiple of two, then jump back using a familiar number pattern. In this case, jumping back from 18 will give nine 2s, so that 19 is nine 2s and one more. Alternatively, jumping forward in 2s from zero to a close number will help in relating multiplication and division, or division questions can be answered using multiplication facts already known. The idea of a remainder is complex and will need to be explored in a number of ways, including sharing and grouping with objects, and on a number line. What to do with the remainder will depend on the context of the problem and children will need to discuss appropriate solutions, not just numerical answers.

## Making connections

By displaying related jumps, such as jumps of 2 and jumps of 4 on the same number line, connections can begin to be made and explanations attempted by the children. They may have already noticed in the number patterns that the multiples of four are always multiples of 2, and representing these facts on an empty number line can provide a visual image to support their explanation.

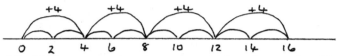

**Figure 5.7** Making connections between multiples of two and multiples of four.

Jumps of 2 and jumps of 3 on a number line can lead to an illustration where the multiples of 6 appear in both patterns. These idea can be reinforced by the game 'Fizz-Buzz' as the oral patterns are explored. In this game the whole class can take turns as they count in ones, but replacing every multiple of 2 by the word 'fizz' and every multiple of 3 by 'buzz'. Multiples of 6 will then become 'fizz-buzz'. The connections that are made between different multiples will help children in developing flexible approaches to more complex calculations with multiplication and division, in particular, doubling and halving methods that will be discussed in the next chapter.

## Extending use of the empty number line

It has been suggested earlier in this chapter that locating decimals on the empty number line can prove a challenging activity that focuses on the extension of the place value number system.

Initially working between 0 and 1, the numbers 0.1 to 0.9 can be located on a 'zoomed in' version, and then mixed numbers such as 2.7 or 1.9 can be located. As well as illustrating the meaning of tenths, this can provide a visual image that helps when 'rounding' numbers, whether decimals or whole numbers. What is needed when a number such as 4.7 is rounded to the nearest whole number, is the closest whole number on the number line. At a later stage, extension to two places of decimals can be related to systems of measurement, such as metres and centimetres, or pounds and pence. Care must be taken as confusion will arise when a number such as 1.60 is identified as 'one point sixty' rather than 'one and six-tenths'. This can lead to the erroneous identification of 1.60 and 1.6 as different when in fact they are representations of the same number.

Identifying the location of fractions is a further activity on the empty number line, and this imagery can help in finding equivalence. Starting with 1 as the numerator, the positions of fractions ½, ¼, and so on, can be shown. This will illustrate how the size of the *denominator* (the number on the bottom) is inversely proportional to the size of the fraction and all these unit fractions are crammed into a very short part of the number line. Introducing different *numerators* (the number on top) while keeping the denominator the same will show how these fractions extend along the whole number line, including the fraction form of whole numbers and mixed numbers.

Illustrating fractions and decimals on the same number line shows the equivalent forms of numbers. These forms can also be related to percentages as the three systems – percentages, decimals and fractions – provide different representations of the same numbers (Figure 5.8).

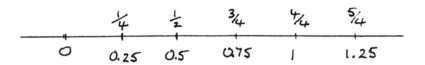

**Figure 5.8**   Decimal and fraction equivalence.

Although it has been traditional to start with fractions and then extend to equivalent decimals and to percentages, alternative approaches have been researched. Moss and Case (1999) report a successful teaching experiment beginning with percentages rather than fractions and decimals. Their justification was to 'capitalize on children's pre-existing knowledge' of whole numbers and to postpone 'the problem of having to compare and manipulate ratios'. With the number line image, children can develop flexibility and choose which system to work in when it comes to comparing numbers and combining them. The importance of this ability to work with equivalent representations is shown in the following quote from the Qualifications and Curriculum Authority:

> Children need an understanding of how fractions, decimals and percentages relate to each other. For example, if they know that ½, 0.5 and 50% are all ways of representing the same part of a whole, then the calculations
>
> $$½ \times 40$$
> $$40 \times 0.5$$
> $$50\% \text{ of } £40$$
>
> can be seen as different versions of the same calculation.
>
> (QCA, 1999, p. 52)

## Activities

1. Illustrate on an empty number line three different ways for doing each of the following calculations:
   185 + 46
   185 − 46
   185 − 97
2. Discuss what are the particular characteristics of a calculation that invite different empty number line strategies, such as bridging through tens, or compensating.

# CHAPTER 6

# Multiplication and Division

When children initially develop strategies for multiplication and division they already know about addition and subtraction and will begin by relating each new operation to things they already know. Early experiences will not involve the mathematical symbols but need to introduce a range of practical situations that will help to establish meanings for the vocabulary associated with the operations. Words like 'multiply' and 'divide' are not found in everyday conversation but will formalize a variety of words that are used to describe multiplicative situations, such as 'lots of', 'each', 'times' and 'share'.

Greer (1992) identifies four main categories of practical situation that involve the multiplication of whole numbers:

- equivalent groups (e.g. 3 tables, each with 4 children);
- multiplicative comparison (*scale factor*) (e.g. 3 times as many boys as girls);
- rectangular arrays (e.g. 3 rows of 4 children); and
- cartesian product (e.g. the number of different possibilities for girl–boy pairs from 3 girls and 4 boys).

Each of these situation can be associated with particular ways of asking a question, and each may be represented in a way that shows *repeated sets, many-to-one* correspondence, an *array* of rows and columns, and a *many-to-many* correspondence, respectively (Figure 6.1).

These situations all involve three numbers in a mathematical relationship: the number of objects in each set, the number of sets and the total number. For multiplication it is the total number that is missing but if either of the other two numbers is to be found division is introduced. For division either the number of groups, or the number in each group, can be missing. It is therefore possible to identify two distinct types of division:

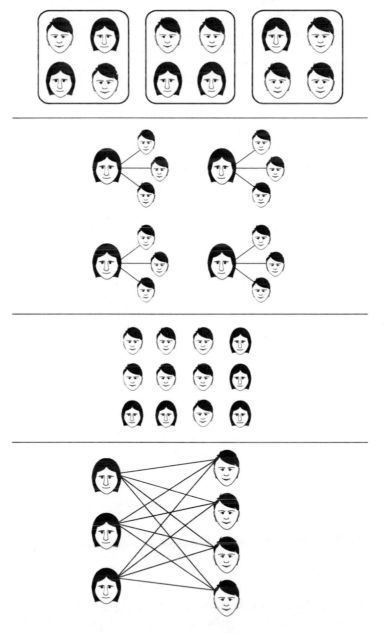

**Figure 6.1** *Repeated sets, many-to-one correspondence,* an *array* of rows and columns, and a *many-to-many correspondence.*

- measurement/grouping (*quotitive*) (e.g. 12 children at tables of 4, how many tables?); and
- sharing (*partitive*) (e.g. 12 children at 4 tables, how many at each?)

It will be important for children to think about multiplication and division in all these different ways and to appreciate that they may all be related to the same numerical calculations. Although each of the situations above suggest actions that could be used to solve a problem, it is the understanding of abstract relationships between numbers that will encourage efficient approaches. It is then that children realize a calculation procedure does not need to reflect the structure of the problem to be solved.

## Early experiences

Although multiplication is introduced first in school, the actions of sharing and grouping are probably more familiar. Research has shown that children as young as four years old are capable of performing dividing procedures in some situations with concrete materials (Pepper and Hunting, 1998). As early as kindergarten, children can model both grouping and sharing division problems with objects (Carpenter *et al.*, 1993; Kouba and Franklin, 1995). The process of formalizing these ideas involves the introduction of precise language and a focus on the number relationships that are generated. Nunes and Bryant (1996) distinguish between the *action* of sharing and the *operation* of division, because understanding division involves a diversity of situations beyond the actions of sharing. In contrast to sharing, removing equal groups from a set of objects more directly shows that repeated subtraction breaks down a set, reversing the way multiplication builds up a set from equal groups.

Nunes and Bryant (1996) suggest that the simplest form of multiplicative situation that children will meet is probably one in which there is a *one-to-many correspondence* between two sets (e.g. 1 car with 4 wheels) which relates to a *ratio*, or *scale factor*, and is the basis for multiplicative, rather than additive thinking. They contrast this with *repeated addition*, which they refer to as *replicating*, but they suggest that replication is not like *joining* (for addition), where any two sets of objects can be combined to give a new set of the same types of objects. Multiplication relates to two numbers, each having a different role (the number in each set and a tally for the number of sets), which need to be coordinated in a way that is more complex than addition. Collecting 5 sets of 4 wheels will require each set of 4 objects to be counted as individual items *and* the same objects collected into sets as the sets themselves are counted. This relates to the size of jumps and the number of equal jumps on an empty number line (see Chapter 5).

Early experiences involve children in learning to count sets as well as counting individual objects. Partitioning and regrouping objects in equal sets will help to establish the language and numerical relationships that will be the foundation for later calculations. Even where children work confidently with numbers, the abstraction needed to appreciate the way three numbers relate in multiplication and division is not as immediately clear as the relationship generated when two sets are combined in addition. Gray and Tall (1994) suggest that the introduction of multiplication and division can present a 'proceptual divide' between those who can and cannot integrate these new ideas within their existing understanding. They note that there can be a cumulative effect of new operations and multiplication and division ideas will be almost impossible for some children to coordinate while they are having problems with addition and subtraction.

## Number patterns and inverse operations

Links between the different arithmetic operations can be established by expressing the same results in different ways. The operation '2 add 2 add 2' can be expressed as '3 lots of 2' or '3 times 2'. By asking the question 'How many lots of 2 make 6?', the idea of division is introduced as the inverse of multiplication. These ideas are related to counting in twos, '2, 4, 6', and equal jumps on a number line as described in the last chapter. Getting children to extend these ideas to '4 lots of 2' and '5 lots of 2' by counting in twos and showing this on a number line will support a mental strategy that is helpful for calculating and which will help them to be less reliant on manipulating the actual materials.

With such small numbers it is not always clear to children that multiplication is introducing a new and powerful operation and some will continue to rely on addition to solve problems (Anghileri, 1995b). When large numbers are introduced, such as the multiples of 20, the distinction between '3 add 20' and '3 lots of 20' introduces a bigger contrast that can illustrate more clearly that multiplication is a distinct operation for recording.

## Remainders

In their experiences children will find that some numbers will not relate quite so neatly to equal groupings, for example seven objects cannot be grouped exactly in twos and will involve objects that are 'left over'. This can be the focus for discussion as 'seven is not in the pattern of counting in twos' or 'seven is only one more than six', as number sense is developed to reason about the numbers involved. Again, these ideas can be associated with patterns on a number line when equal jumps are taken and not all numbers are 'landed on'. Rather than isolating multiplication and division, connections between the numbers and the operations will help develop the 'feel' for numbers that is so important. Ask any adult what happens when 13 objects are to be shared between 4 people and there will be no need to refer to any sharing procedure as 13 is a familiar number that is easily related to 12, which is a multiple of 4. Such familiarity with numbers will develop when children progress from practical activities to talking about and recording relationships among the numbers.

## Learning the patterns

From counting in twos, fives and tens (sometimes referred to as 'skip' counting) children can be encouraged to learn the number patterns for other numbers, including multiples of 20, 100 or 15, extending them as far as they can. Stages in developing such patterns take children from counting every one, to internalizing the interim numbers, and then using only multiples (Anghileri, 1995b). Through ideas of equal groupings, children develop new counting patterns where some numbers are emphasized more than others (e.g. 1, 2, *3*, 4, 5, *6*, 7, 8, *9* ...). This involves a concurrent count as each triple of numbers is monitored and a *rhythm* is very helpful to maintain the pattern of three each time. The interim numbers are then left out altogether and knowing this counting pattern already reduces to two the concurrent counts that need to be kept. This is where an empty number line is helpful as only the pattern numbers need be represented with the location of other numbers imagined. Where children are using this strategy to calculate a given multiple, say 6 threes, a third concurrent count will be needed to tally the number of threes and children can sometimes be seen using their fingers to keep this tally (see Chapter 2) or can use an empty number line and count the jumps. Knowing these counting sequences is not yet enough for understanding multiplication and division but it brings familiarity to 'families' of numbers and rapid recall of such patterns will be helpful in later calculations. It is very powerful, where multiplication and division are concerned, to have a 'sense' that the number 16 relates well to 2 and 4 and 8, but not so well related to 5 or to 3.

Teaching number sense involves helping children to understand that multiplication and division can both be related to the same number patterns and that it is these number relationships that will provide the ultimate key to successful calculating.

## Diversity in meanings

The situations identified above all relate to whole numbers and this is the way the operations will first be introduced. In developing number sense, identifying multiplication only as repeated addition, and division only as sharing, will impose limitations for children by making the interpretation of some later calculations impossible, for example, $0.3 \times 0.4$ and $12 \div \frac{1}{2}$ (Anghileri, 1995a). In order to extend the meanings to include these types of calculation, the idea of a *ratio* between pairs of numbers is used, for example with pattern of numbers 0, 1, 2, 3 ... associated with 0, 4, 8, 12 (4 times). This type of ratio can be developed to reflect relationships between numbers that are not integers, for example 0, 1, 2, 3 ... associated with 0, 0.2, 0.4, 0.6 ... (Figure 6.2).

Using this idea of a ratio, multiplying by a number smaller than 1 can be identified with division, for example, finding one third of a group of 12 by dividing by 3.

89

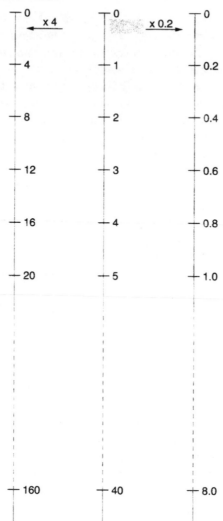

**Figure 6.2** Number lines showing '4 times' and '0.2 times'.

## Introducing the multiplication symbol

The multiplication symbol can be introduced as a succinct way of writing repeated addition and, as such, will be a welcome shorthand for recording some of the facts that children have known for some time. Although multiples of 2 are usually the first family of facts to be introduced, the real value of the shorthand notation is not immediately obvious (2 + 2 is little different from 2 × 2) and confusion is quite common. Greater motivation for the new symbol can be achieved if its efficiency is clearer, and starting with multiples of 25 can be fun, as well as giving purpose for using the new symbol.

Confusion can also develop about the way multiplication is written, as 3 × 25 and 25 × 3 are often interpreted in exactly the same way. It is sometimes argued that the 'correct' way of reading 3 × 25 is '3 multiplied by 25', that is, three taken twenty-five times or 3 + 3 + 3 + ... + 3 + 3. This fits with the other operations where addition, subtraction and division 'operate on' the first number with the second but flexibility in interpretation will lead to sensible choices.

The 'everyday' interpretation of 3 × 25 as '3 times 25', that is, twenty-five taken three times or 25 + 25 + 25, may be more sensible in this case for calculating purposes. The word 'times' provides an appropriate alternative to 'multiplied by' as long as teachers are aware that hesitation by children may arise from the ambiguity involved. What is important is that children are able to make appropriate choices in identifying a meaning for the symbols and a procedure for calculating. This can be shown in the alternative interpretations of expressions such as 2 × 50 (2 lots of 50) and ½ × 4 (4 lots of ½).

## The commutative rule

The reason that different verbal interpretations are equally valid is the *commutative rule* which says that 2 × 50 = 50 × 2 as both will give the same numerical result. Since the images of '50 lots of 2' and '2 lots of 50' are quite different (and their equivalent representations as jumps on a number line give no clue to the reason why they are equal), it may take some time for children to use the commutative rule effectively.

$$50 + 50 = 2 + 2 + 2 + 2 + 2 \dots \text{fifty times.}$$

Research has shown that experiences of repeated addition, particularly where there are only images of repeated sets, impose limits on developing mathematical ideas involving commutativity (Schlieman *et al.*, 1998). Working with street vendors with little schooling and with school pupils, they found that specific teaching plays an important role in developing the ability to use commutativity in solving multiplication problems. Nunes *et al.* (1993) showed that even nine- and ten-year-old school children did not easily accept the commutative rule when they tried to solve context problems, such as calculating '14 lots of 3 dollars', and the structure of equal groups within the problems was influential in determining what number was to be repeatedly added. The commutative rule is important in establishing the flexibility needed to find the most efficient calculation strategy for any given problem.

One of the ways that the commutative rule can be investigated as a more abstract principle is by using an *array* and providing children with opportunities to arrange and rearrange sets of objects (Figure 6.3).

**Figure 6.3** An array showing '5 lots of 3' and '3 lots of 5'.

Moving objects into rows and columns will provide better opportunities to explore the commutative rule than static pictures which are sometimes difficult to see in the two different ways (as rows of one number, and at the same time columns of another number). Acceptance of the commutative rule marks progression from understanding multiplication only as repeated addition, to multiplicative approaches that relate to other types of problem; *scale factor* problems, for example a bicycle travelling 8 times as fast as a pedestrian, and *cartesian product* problems, for example the number of sandwiches that can be selected using 3 types of bread and 4 types of filling, both involve multiplication that is not so evidently repeated addition (Murray *et al.*, 1991; Mulligan and Mitchelmore, 1997).

## Introducing the division symbol

As with multiplication, the division symbol may be introduced as a shorthand way of recording results already known, but the way to interpret the division symbol can cause difficulties that may not be evident in the earlier stages. The problem '600 ÷ 6' can be interpreted as 'how many lots of 6 make 600?' related to the count 6, 12, 18 ... or can be interpreted as '6 lots of what make 600?' which may lead to an easier solution. These interpretations may be identified with the 'repeated subtraction' and 'sharing' and show the importance of children being flexible in their interpretation of division. The interpretation of a problem such as 8 ÷ ¼ will be virtually impossible if the only interpretation is one of sharing (8 shared by ¼ of a person?). Children who do not have the flexibility to match an appropriate interpretation to a symbolic problem will be hampered in their progress to these calculations. Division does not obey the commutative rule although many children will attempt to use it when they meet a problem such as 4 ÷ 8 (Anghileri, 1995a, 1998). Early introduction to problems such as '4 shared between 8' in practical situations, discussing its contrast with '8 shared between 4', will show that smaller numbers *can* be divided by bigger ones, avoiding the misconception that 'division always makes smaller' (Fischbein *et al.*, 1985).

## Reinforcing the importance of number triple

The most effective ways of calculating will become established when children recognize that multiplication and division both determine a number triple which may be identified independently of any practical procedure. The number 24, for example, is related to 3 and 8 in a way that involves both multiplication and division. This is reinforced by using the terms *factors* to identify two numbers that are combined by multiplication to give the result which is called the *product*.

---

24 has 3 and 8 as two of its *factors*

24 is the *product* of 3 and 8

This relationship is expressed in four ways using the symbols ' × ' and '÷'

$3 \times 8 = 24,\ 8 \times 3 = 24,\ 24 \div 3 = 8,\ 24 \div 8 = 3$

---

The term *divisor* of a number is an alternative to 'factor', used to identify any whole number that divides exactly into it without a remainder, for example 1, 2, 3, 4, 6 and 12 are all the factors/divisors of 12. A corresponding term is the *multiple* of a number which refers to any numbers obtained by multiplication, for example 6, 9, 12 ... are all the multiples of 3. By recording multiplication and division facts together, and relating results to number patterns, children will gain a better sense not only of the number relationships that are involved with a number and its factors, but also the relationships that exist between the operations.

## Learning the facts

Traditionally, learning 'times tables' has taken up a considerable amount of time in primary school. For some children this is an efficient way for them to achieve immediate recall of those isolated facts that they will need when calculating. For some children, however, the task of memorizing so many facts becomes unmanageable, and alternative strategies must be found for enabling them to calculate rapidly. Not only are the facts difficult to memorize, but the isolation sometimes imposed by learning 'times tables' can inhibit children in using multiplicative methods to solve problems. Even in the later years in primary school some children persist with very primitive methods like tallying and repeated addition to calculate with large numbers (Anghileri, 1999) where they are unsure of the ways multiplicative facts can be applied.

Chanting and rote learning can be helpful for learning some of

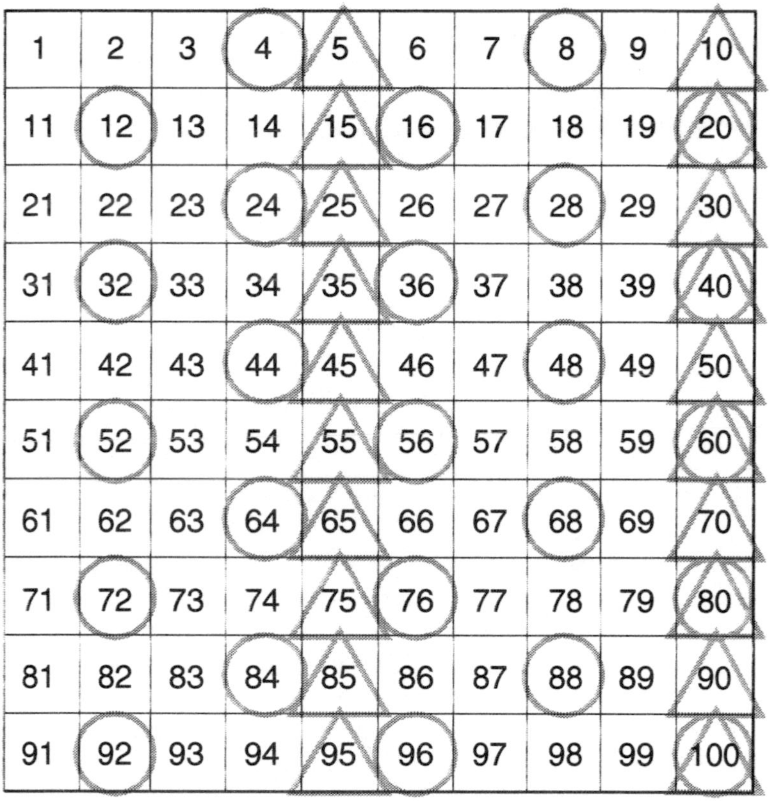

| 1 | 2 | 3 | 4 | 5 | 6 | 7 | 8 | 9 | 10 |
|---|---|---|---|---|---|---|---|---|----|
| 11 | 12 | 13 | 14 | 15 | 16 | 17 | 18 | 19 | 20 |
| 21 | 22 | 23 | 24 | 25 | 26 | 27 | 28 | 29 | 30 |
| 31 | 32 | 33 | 34 | 35 | 36 | 37 | 38 | 39 | 40 |
| 41 | 42 | 43 | 44 | 45 | 46 | 47 | 48 | 49 | 50 |
| 51 | 52 | 53 | 54 | 55 | 56 | 57 | 58 | 59 | 60 |
| 61 | 62 | 63 | 64 | 65 | 66 | 67 | 68 | 69 | 70 |
| 71 | 72 | 73 | 74 | 75 | 76 | 77 | 78 | 79 | 80 |
| 81 | 82 | 83 | 84 | 85 | 86 | 87 | 88 | 89 | 90 |
| 91 | 92 | 93 | 94 | 95 | 96 | 97 | 98 | 99 | 100 |

**Figure 6.4**  Multiplication patterns on a 100 square.

the facts, and most children will be successful in learning the 'zero' and 'one times tables' which both hold important initial facts. Alternatively, the identification of patterns on a hundred square will provide visual images that can help them to reconstruct those facts that are not immediately remembered (Figure 6.4).

The most important aspect of learning multiplication facts is the way each fact is related to a whole lot of others. Knowing '3 fours are 12', for example, should give rapid access to '6 fours' by doubling. As it appears to be easier to recall '7 sevens' than '8 sevens', adding one more seven onto 49 will be a better strategy than reciting the whole 'table' in the hope of jogging the memory. Making connections among the facts will not only minimize the

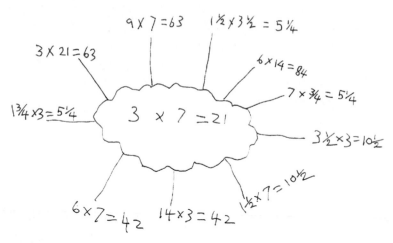

**Figure 6.5** A web showing results connected with 3 × 7.

number of facts to be learned but will encourage strategies that will reduce the working in later calculations (Figure 6.5). Doubling and halving are important preparations and as soon as a few facts are learned the emphasis can be transferred to all the connected facts that can be derived.

When the commutative rule is known, the number of facts to be learned is immediately halved. *Understanding how to make the links is as important as memorizing the facts.*

Counting in twos, threes or fives is too often dismissed as irrelevant to classroom practice but children are often familiar with such patterns of numbers and they are important for developing number sense. They will provide a strategy for calculating that extends well beyond the limited facts in the 'tables', and chanting in 'fives', for example, shows a clear pattern in the numbers up to and beyond 100. Where a tally is kept (often with fingers) children have rapid access to a means of calculating with which they are secure and confident. Extending the counting pattern of twos to the patterns for four (only say every other number) will reinforce the connections and provide another access to number facts. Showing jumps in twos and in fours on the same number line will give an image of the way these patterns relate to each other and children can be encouraged to explain the connections they can see. Immediate access to as many multiplication and division facts as possible is desirable (for example, $3 \times 15$, $4 \times 25$) but undue emphasis on 'times tables' will not achieve the aim of getting children to use these facts appropriately.

## Extending the multiplication and division facts to multiples and powers of ten

Extending the multiplication facts to include multiples of ten (20, 30 ...) and powers of ten (100, 1000 ... and later 0.1) needs to be given some meaning as these will be an important part of strategies for multiplying larger numbers. Careful development of such ideas is necessary if children are to work with understanding rather than rules they have memorized. Multiplying by ten or one hundred is not a case of 'adding noughts' (this will fail when 0.5 is multiplied by ten!) but can be explained by repeated addition and the commutative rule, or explored on a calculator. At the same time, division by tens and hundreds can be related to these facts, using the idea that multiplication and division are inverse operations that 'undo' each other.

## Developing understanding in stages

To retain understanding while developing ideas involving multiples and powers of ten, a variety of contexts are needed, such as working with money, measures, structured apparatus and calculators. This will introduce imagery that can help children to make sense of the abstract calculations. Ideas can be extended progressively introducing some of the rules of arithmetic. The following possible stages are illustrated for $40 \times 3$, $400 \times 3$ and $40 \times 30$:

- *Stage 1*: Using repeated addition and the *commutative rule.*
  Initially, $10 + 10 + 10 = 30$ is identified with *3 lots of ten*, and this is associated with *10 lots of threes*, both making 30.
  Now *3 lots of forty* and *40 lots of three* can be identified with $40 + 40 + 40 = 120$ and can be written as $40 \times 3 = 120$ or as $3 \times 40 = 120$.
  At the same time this relates to $120 \div 30 = 4$ and $120 \div 4 = 30$.

(Some children may like to see this verified with a simple calculator, keying in 3, +, + and pressing the '=' button 40 times. Appropriate questions such as 'Will the display show 50, or 100?' can make this an opportunity to become more familiar with multiples of 3.)

Extending this idea, '400 lots of 3' is the same as '3 lots of 400' and is associated with the four calculations: $400 \times 3 = 1200$, $3 \times 400 = 1200$, $1200 \div 400 = 3$ and $1200 \div 3 = 400$.

- *Stage 2*: Linking known facts and using the *associative rule*.

  The *associative rule* allows the numbers to be paired in a different way and then combined by multiplication, for example, $3 \times (4 \times 10) = (3 \times 4) \times 10$.

  Using the idea that $\times 40$ is the same as $\times 4$ followed by $\times 10$ allows $3 \times 40$ to be calculated as $(3 \times 4) \times 10 = 12 \times 10$.

  When multiples of 100 are known, $3 \times 400$ can be calculated as $(3 \times 4) \times 100$.

- *Stage 3*: Both numbers as multiples of ten.

  The calculation $30 \times 40$ can be thought of as 30 lots of 40 or 40 lots of 30 but repeated addition will be inefficient. Using the associative rule can involve known facts:

  $30 \times 40 = 30 \times (4 \times 10) = (30 \times 4) \times 10 = 120 \times 10 = 1200$

  or

  $30 \times 40 = (3 \times 10) \times 40 = 3 \times (10 \times 40) = 3 \times 400 = 1200$.

  Using both the associative and commutative rule the result can be calculated as:

  $(3 \times 10) \times (4 \times 10) = (3 \times 4) \times (10 \times 10) = 12 \times 100$.

  The equivalent division problems would give $1200 \div 30 = 40$ and $1200 \div 40 = 30$.

It cannot be overemphasized that the power in calculating lies in appreciating the patterns that are generated in this way. Children need encouragement to explore different combinations of numbers including multiples and powers of ten, and to talk about their findings so that the results themselves become familiar and a result such as $12 \times 100$ is 'known' rather than calculated.

A calculator provides a quick and reliable way to observe

patterns like the effect of multiplying by ten. Rousham describes an activity in which groups of children would write down a list of numbers of their choice ('your age, your door number ... a big number, a small number ...') and look for any patterns they might find. He claims that the calculator makes the activity more powerful because of the range of numbers and quantity of results that can be seen.

> The entire number system is built into a calculator, place value particularly, and by using it a lot, much incidental information about how numbers behave and are changed by the various operations is absorbed in a way that is qualitatively different from working with the printed page
>
> (Rousham, 1999, p. 95)

He goes on to talk of the 'fierce interest in patterns, numbers and how they behave' as the children had the opportunity to investigate more and more numbers and retain control of the ideas they were exploring. With the calculators they gained experiences with many different numbers and the way they are related using multiplication and division. This provides more powerful strategies for calculating than procedures that are abstractions from manipulating concrete materials.

## Mental strategies for multiplying larger numbers

Multiplication of larger numbers involves 'breaking' the calculation into smaller parts and there are many ways this may be done. Where repeated addition is inefficient, more efficient 'chunks' can be used without losing understanding of the fundamental idea. The multiplication $3 \times 26$, for example, could be calculated as '3 lots of 20 together with 3 lots of 6' or it could be '3 lots of 25 and 3 more' and each of these calculations relates to a different way of 'chunking' the number 26 to relate to already established facts. The strategies that allow a calculation to be re-organized can be recorded in 'jottings' and addressed explicitly in discussions. Children will develop effective approaches and appropriate mathematical language by contrasting and comparing their different approaches under the guidance of a teacher. The teacher's role will be to help them organize their informal recordings and make explicit the rules and conventions that underpin effective approaches.

Formally, both of the approaches above use the *distributive rule* that enables a multiplication to be 'distributed' over the sum of two parts:

$$3 \times 26 = 3 \times (20 + 6) = (3 \times 20) + (3 \times 6) = 60 + 18$$

or

$$3 \times (25 + 1) = (3 \times 25) + (3 \times 1) = 75 + 3$$

(Children need to know these results but not the name for the rule.)

This particular calculation could also have been tackled using a doubling and halving strategy as $3 \times 26 = 6 \times 13$ which is '6 twelves and 6 more' and this would result in different jottings. Children may enjoy finding as many ways as possible to do such a calculation and different ways to record their findings with the emphasis on gaining efficiency and devising clear recording methods.

When two-digit numbers are to be multiplied by two-digit numbers, mental strategies may need to be supported with pencil and paper. At this stage children will benefit from discussions which introduce a variety of methods. Sometimes the structure of a problem may suggest an approach but the calculation may or may not reflect this structure. Take, for example, the problem: 'For the school fete, 24 children will each make 16 cakes. How many cakes altogether?' Although the context suggests 24 lots of 16, the calculation $24 \times 16$ can be approached as 24 lots of 16 or as 16 lots of 24.

| 24 lots of 16 | 16 lots of 24 |
|---|---|
| (20 lots of 16) + (4 lots of 16) | (10 lots of 24) + (6 lots of 24) |
| (24 lots of 10) + (24 lots of 6) | (16 lots of 20) + (16 lots of 4) |

Multiplication by a two-digit number can be avoided altogether if this problem is transformed by doubling and halving:

$$24 \times 16 = 48 \times 8 = 96 \times 4 = 192 \times 2 = 200 + 180 + 4 = 384$$

Such a method demonstrates the way connections may be made between calculations when a standard approach to recording is delayed. Perhaps the most elegant solution to this particular problem would be using the 'fact' that $25 \times 16 = 400$ and then subtracting 16 from 400.

It is important for individual pupils to identify a way of thinking about how any problem may be tackled, and the stages that need to be recorded. Starting with 'long hand' notes, explaining the method, and structuring some written recording, are all part of the development of understanding. Some pupils will work quickly towards a concise ways to record their work but some may need time to work with extended forms of recording in order for steps in the calculation to be meaningful.

## Division with numbers beyond the tables facts

In the same way that multiplication of bigger numbers involves choices about the way a problem may be tackled, the same is true for division. Depending on the way a calculation is interpreted, a problem such as $96 \div 4$ is seen as sharing (96 shared between 4) or repeated subtraction (how many fours in 96?). Both methods may be developed to greater efficiency where 'chunks' of increasing size can be related to known facts (Anghileri, 2000, 2004). Dividing 96 by 4 may involve 'sharing' 10 at a time into 4 sets until 80 of the 96 have been 'used', the remaining 16 giving a further 4 each, so that 24 each is the result (Figure 6.6).

Using repeated subtraction this calculation can also be done by 'chunking' the 96 into numbers that are associated with four, for example, $96 = 40 + 40 + 16$, with '10 lots of 4' and '10 lots of 4' and then '4 lots of 4'. Recognizing that 80 and 16 are appropriate 'chunks' will lead to a more efficient calculation. The recognition of related 'chunks' for a calculation will often involve multiples of ten, for example 10 lots of 4, or 20 lots of 4, and provides a strategy that will extend to any size divisor. Just as multiplication 'builds up' numbers in stages, division can be seen as 'breaking down' numbers in equivalent stages. In this way division is reinforced as the inverse operation to multiplication.

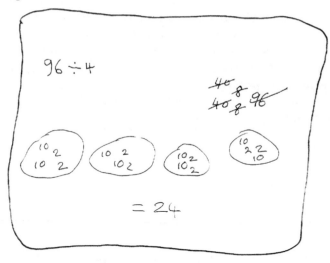

**Figure 6.6**   96 ÷ 4 by sharing ten at a time.

## Division with two-digit divisors

For division by a two-digit divisor there are various methods including the traditional long division algorithm which will be discussed in the next chapter. Pupils will need to decide on the most effective approach for each problem they meet and some calculations will be best undertaken with a calculator. In some types of problem, number sense will play an important role where children select an approach that best suits the numbers involved. Take, for example, the problem 64 ÷ 16. This problem cannot easily be solved using a traditional algorithm but as a repeated subtraction (how many 16s are in 64?) the solution is easier. The fact that pupils are familiar with the numbers 64 and 16, and relate then with the numbers 4 and 8, will be helpful in suggesting that a doubling or halving approach can be used to solve the problem. Adults will recognize the greater complexity involved in calculating 63 ÷ 17 even before any strategy is attempted. It is this 'feel' for numbers and the associations they evoke that makes the difference between children who are confident in their calculation methods and those that attempt only to follow procedures they have been taught (Anghileri, 2001b, 2004).

102

## Informal approaches and 'messy' working

When working within a context, the structure of a problem can influence the strategy used to find a solution. Although some children become able to select a method independent of the problem type, but which best suits the numbers, there is evidence that other pupils find it difficult to know what is the connection between the mathematics previously taught and the context of the problem (Clarke and Kamii, 1996). Rather than using number facts they have learned to solve the problems effectively, these pupils fall back on inefficient methods such as tallying or counting in ones (Figure 6.7).

1256 apples are divided among 6 shopkeepers. How many apples will every shopkeeper get? How many apples will be left?

**Figure 6.7**   An inefficient method for calculating.

Children's jottings or personal records will give teachers insight into the way problems are approached and the extent to which individuals are abstracting an arithmetic operation from the reality of a given problem.

Doubling and halving are often seen in children's informal

432 children have to be transported by
15-seater buses.
–How many buses will be needed?

Figure 6.8   Informal working for 432 ÷ 15.

approaches and, with teacher support, will lead progressively to more efficiency. In using informal approaches, children are able to explore their understanding of a problem and bring to it the facts and strategies they think are relevant (Figure 6.8).

The range of different strategies this will involve provides a good basis for discussion and the children's understanding may be enhanced by talking about their own methods and listening to others. Although the method illustrated lacks the efficiency of a standard algorithm, it is clear that the solution is focused on the problem with the result interpreted to give a realistic answer. Where the calculation becomes purely mechanical, errors in working can result in bizarre answers that are not realistic solutions to the problem (Figure 6.9).

Research has shown that many pupils focus mainly on the mathematics, stop at the point of reaching an arithmetic solution and do not re-interpret their answer in the real context of the problem to check if it is appropriate. A balance has to be achieved between the abstraction that involves selection of the most efficient calculation method, and applications of calculating to real problems.

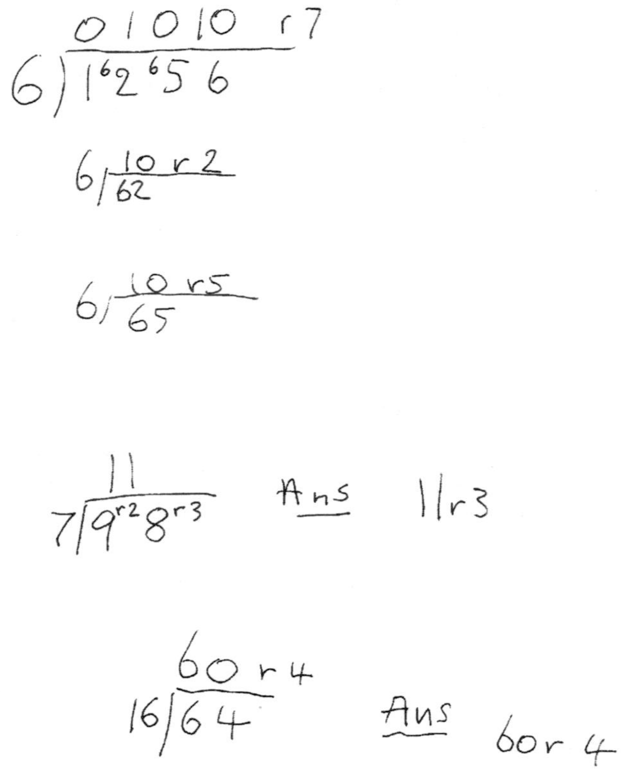

**Figure 6.9** Purely mechanical calculations with unrealistic solutions.

## Activity

1. Use three different written methods for doing the calculation 228 × 32. Use a doubling method for the calculation 228 × 8, and discuss how this could be useful for the calculation 228 × 32.

2. Make up two context problems, one to match the sharing (*partition*) structure of division and one to match the grouping (*quotation*) structure of division. Discuss mental methods that may be used to solve each of these problems.

# CHAPTER 7

# Written Calculations

Pencil and paper recording has been introduced in the previous chapters to support children's informal methods and to establish patterns in the relationships among numbers. This chapter will consider further developments to establish efficient written methods that children can understand and use successfully for numbers of increasing size and complexity.

In identifying the role of written procedures in a society that depends on technology for all important calculations, reservations about the need for *standard* algorithms have been expressed by mathematics educators for many years (Plunkett, 1979; Thompson, 1997; Anghileri, 2001a). A strong view was expressed as long ago as 1979 by Stuart Plunkett:

> The advent of calculators has provided us with a great opportunity. We are freed from the necessity to provide every citizen with methods for dealing with calculations of indefinite complexity. So we can abandon the standard written algorithms, of general applicability and limited intelligibility, in favour of methods more suited to the minds and purposes of the users ... Children should be helped to acquire sensible methods for calculating ... [and] will acquire a better understanding of number from using their own mental algorithms than from the repeated application of standard algorithms they do not comprehend.
>
> (Plunkett, 1979, p. 5)

In his classic article, Plunkett compares standard written methods of calculating with mental methods. He notes that standard written algorithms are *contracted, efficient, automatic, symbolic, analytic* and *generalizable,* but he points out the important disadvantage of the algorithms not being easily grasped by pupils because of their lack of correspondence with informal methods. Mental methods, on the other hand, are *fleeting, variable, flexible, active, holistic* and *constructive,* but overall, *personal* approaches for which the children have ownership. Teaching standardized procedures for calculating, he argues, encourages '*cognitive passivity*' and '*suspended understanding*' as they do not correspond to the way people naturally think about numbers. If the purpose of number work is to develop number sense then the contracted traditional algorithms, that rely on the manipulation of digits in a highly structured spatial arrangement, will be inappropriate for most calculations.

Although standard algorithms have been the focus for much teaching in the past, studies of workplace mathematics have also found that that where pencil and paper methods are used by adults, they are rarely the methods traditionally taught in school (see for example the Cockcroft report, 1982, pp. 19–20). Rather than using formal written procedures, adults frequently use idiosyncratic jottings to support personal methods that are adapted to reflect the structure of the problem and the numbers that are involved. Teaching approaches need to acknowledge the way calculations are tackled 'in real life'. Also, as children have established foundations for calculating mentally it will be important to work progressively from the informal jottings that support mental strategies to more formalised methods so that their confidence and understanding are not jeopardized (Anghileri, 2001a, 2004).

## Children's intuitive approaches

Research has shown that before standard methods are taught in school, children's first approaches to solving numerical problems reflect the understanding they have of each individual situation. Multiplication and division problems, for example, have proved to be interesting operations to study because children already have considerable experiences with numbers that they bring to bear on any problem. In research on children's strategies for solving such problems, Mulligan and Mitchelmore (1997) found that:

> children acquire an expanding repertoire of intuitive models and the model they employ to solve any particular problem reflects the mathematical structure they impose on it.

Even when the algorithms are introduced there is evidence that children persist in employing their own methods with better success. Murray *et al.* (1991) found that children

107

invent powerful non-standard algorithms alongside school-taught algorithms: that they prefer to use their own algorithms when allowed to ... and that their success rate when using their own algorithms is significantly higher than the success rate of children who use the standard algorithms or when they themselves use standard algorithms.

## From informal to formal written methods

The need for pencil and paper will arise where more complex calculations are introduced and some form of written recording is first developed to support mental calculation:

> Through a process of regular explanation and discussion of their own and other children's methods, [pupils] will begin to acquire a repertoire of mental calculation strategies. At this stage, it can be hard for them to hold all the intermediate steps in their heads, and so informal pencil and paper notes, recording some or all of their solutions, become part of a mental strategy.
>
> (DfEE, 1998, p. 109)

Such notes will start as unstructured personal jottings that may be difficult for a teacher or other pupils to decipher. 'These personal jottings may not be easy for someone else to follow, but they are a staging post to getting the right answer and to acquiring fluency in mental calculation' (DfEE, 1998, p. 109).

An empty number line, as described in Chapter 5, can provide a jotting that supports children's thinking and relates calculating to their skills in counting. When larger numbers are involved, pencil and paper recording is necessary for keeping track of a calculation and this may be in the form of informal jottings or as a standard written format. Ruthven (1998) identifies two distinct purposes: 'to augment working memory by *recording* key items of information' and 'to cue sequences of actions through *schematising* such information within a standard spatial configuration' (emphasis in original). The traditional methods that have been taught as algorithms (set procedures for written calculations) may provide the most succinct record, but their contracted form makes them beyond the capabilities of many children at primary school age (van Putten. *et al.*, 2005) and alternative jottings that are used with understanding will be preferable. Pupils will also need to consider when a written method is required, or when a calculator may be most appropriate. In national tests where calculators are allowed it does not make sense to use time in doing a written calculation where the calculator would be quicker.

## Stages in a progression for written recording

Where written recording is introduced for a calculation, there are a variety of methods that follow a progression from mental to part-written, and then to more formally organized written methods that develop efficiency. It is important in the early stages of recording calculations not to introduce the vertical written format before children have had the opportunity to construct different recording methods for themselves. The processes involved in developing their own structured written record provide an important aspect of working mathematically, such as being systematic and clearly communicating their thinking. Although children may enjoy early success with taught algorithms, their contracted nature invites children to work with digits rather than the true values of the numbers and a more mechanical approach can then be applied without understanding (Anghileri, 2001b, 2004).

While the primary purpose for introducing the algorithms has been to 'direct and organize' children's approaches, their formal structure is prone to errors (Brown and Van Lehn, 1980). In analysing these errors it has been shown that children make inappropriate adaptations of the methods they learn as they try to reconstruct a procedure they have not understood and cannot remember. Ruthven and Chaplin (1998) refer to these types of error as 'the improvisation of malgorithms', suggesting that children appear to be following rules, but the wrong rules (Figure 7.1). In many cases the algorithms are difficult to understand as they do not relate to the children's intuitive approaches (Plunkett, 1979; Thompson, 1997; Anghileri, 1998; Anghileri et al., 2002).

Independence from a standard approach will help children to develop confidence in using the number facts that they already know, in approaches that reflect the way they have interpreted the problems. In the early stages, their methods may be long-winded and inefficient but the teacher will be able to help individuals

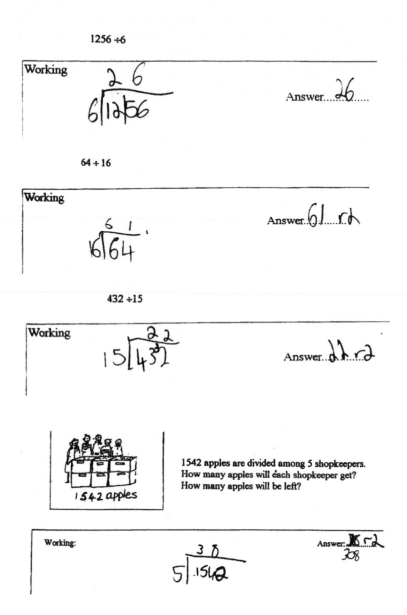

1256 ÷6

Working

Answer....26....

64 ÷ 16

Working

Answer. 61 r0

432 ÷15

Working

Answer. 22 r2

1542 apples are divided among 5 shopkeepers. How many apples will each shopkeeper get? How many apples will be left?

1542 apples

Working:

Answer: 15 r2
308

**Figure 7.1** Errors with the division algorithm.

structure their written records and gain efficiency. By opening up discussion about the best ways to record the working for a given problem, children will gain experience in communicating their ideas both verbally and with the conventional symbols of mathematics. By developing the efficiency and organization of the children's own methods, understanding will not be sacrificed for the sake of efficiency and flexibility and independent thinking will be encouraged so that appropriate methods may be selected for different problems.

## Written methods for addition and subtraction

Mental strategies for addition and subtraction generally reflect two distinct mental approaches that have been described in Chapter 4: the *sequential method* reflecting a counting approach and the *split tens methods* using place value. There are valid forms of formal recording associated with each of these approaches that can be progressively constructed to reflect the mental stages. If confusion is to be avoided, where a child is thinking of a solution strategy along the lines of one of these approaches, the form of written recording needs to reflect this thinking.

## Sequential methods

In sequential methods one of the numbers is retained as a whole and subtotals are found by adding or subtracting parts of the other number as illustrated on the empty number line in Chapter 5. It is arguable that the empty number line presents a highly efficient way to *record* any addition or subtraction calculation and may be the most easily understood by some children.

An alternative recording starts with a horizontal arrangement that reflects the stages in a calculation:

$$58 + 37$$

| | | |
|---|---|---|
| 58 + 2 = 60 | or | 58 + 30 = 88 |
| 60 + 35 = 95 | | 88 + 2 + 5 = 95 |

For subtraction there is the option of counting forwards from the smaller number or counting back from the larger. Again, these result in different written records on the empty number line or in a horizontal format:

$$57 - 38$$

| |
|---|
| 38 + 2 = 40 |
| 40 + 17 = 57 |
| so 57 − 38 = 17 + 2 = 19 |

or

| |
|---|
| 57 − 30 = 27 |
| 27 − 8 = 27 − 7 − 1 = 19 |

These methods have the advantage that all stages in the process are transparent and build on children's knowledge of the ways numbers can be split into convenient 'chunks' so that known number facts can be used.

## Split tens methods

Split tens methods involve the partitioning of both numbers and finding subtotals based on place value. Initially it will be best for children to become familiar with a number such as 58 partitioned into '50 and 8' rather than '5 tens and 8 units' as discussed in earlier chapters.

Just as the empty number line provides an image that will help children to visualize the sequential methods (Figure 7.2), there are images that can help illustrate split tens methods:

| 50 | | 30 | | 80 |
|---|---|---|---|---|
| (58) | + | (37) | = | (95) |
| 8 | | 7 | | 15 |

Thompson (1997) argues that to narrow the gap between children's idiosyncratic mental calculation methods and the traditional vertical written algorithms, a holistic approach may be used that reflects more closely the actual quantities, rather than work with digits. He identifies a partitioning algorithm that builds vertical recording on the mental strategy he refers to as 'a *partial sum* approach', using place value but working with whole numbers rather than digits:

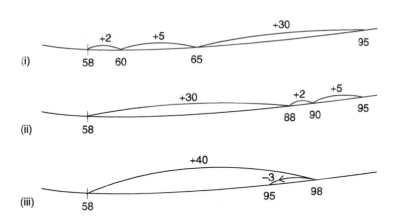

**Figure 7.2** Different methods for calculating 58 + 37 on an empty number line.

```
      5 8
  +   3 7
      8 0
      1 5
      9 5
```

This procedure works from left to right, again reinforcing the way children may think about the problem.

An alternative written method is suggested for children who use a *cumulo-partial* approach:

```
      5 0
  +   3 0
      8 0
  +     8
      8 8
  +     7
      9 5
```

Again, this works with whole numbers and the recording shows all the stages involved. Each of these methods is rather more extended than the traditional algorithm but reflects more closely the mental methods that children are known to use. For some children it may be appropriate to move to more efficiency with part of the calculation done in the head, or with the small reminders, in the style of a traditional algorithm. The aids to memory may take many different forms and different options should be available according to those which are most easily understood by the children themselves:

|  |  |  |  |  |  |  |  |
|---|---|---|---|---|---|---|---|
|   | 5 8 |   | 5 8 |   | 5 8 |   | 5 8 |
| + | 3 7 | + | 3 7 | + | ₁3 7 | + | 3 7 |
|   | 9 5 |   | 9 5 |   | 9 5 |   | 9 5 |
|   | 1 5 |   | 1 |   |   |   | 10 |

It is important that children do not lose the sense in what they are doing and the reasonableness of the result for each calculation.

In a similar way to addition, Thompson suggests an expanded notation for subtraction:

|  |  |  |  |
|---|---|---|---|
| 732 | 700 + 30 + 2 | → | 600 + 120 + 12 |
| −476 | −400 + 70 + 6 |   | − 400 + 70 + 6 |
| 256 |  |   | 200 + 50 + 6 |

Unlike the addition methods, it will be necessary to work from right to left as the units introduce the immediate problem involved in subtracting a larger number (6) from a smaller number (2). There are many stages in this method which still do not appear explicitly and understanding will depend on individuals being confident to 'decompose' the number 732 as 600 + 120 + 12. This is equivalent to the standard algorithm using decomposition but differs by keeping all the numbers whole rather than working with digits that have to be carefully aligned.

114

traditional decomposition algorithm:

$$
\begin{array}{ccc}
{}^{6}\not7 & {}^{12}\not8 & {}^{1}2 \\
- \quad 4 & 7 & 6 \\
\hline
2 & 5 & 6 \\
\end{array}
$$

If children are to build on their established understanding of subtraction then an approach that fits more readily with the mental strategies they have developed for smaller numbers would be to 'count up from 476 to 732' or to 'count down from 732 to 476'. Both of these may be recorded using an empty number line and it is arguable that this will be the most efficient written method for some children (Figure 7.3).

732 – 476

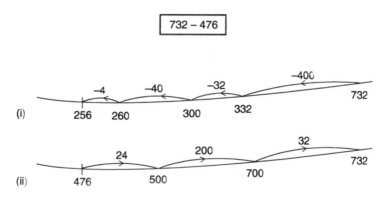

**Figure 7.3** An empty number line to show 732 − 476.

The question must be asked about what is the purpose of the calculation. As discussed in the introduction to this book, if the purpose is to find the solution to a particular problem using an efficient and reliable method then individual children should be encouraged to use any method that they are confident fits this requirement. On some occasions they may be encouraged to use a more traditional method that reflects the place value structure of the numbers. Whatever method is required the objective should be made explicit and the choices available to the children made clear.

Thompson offers some more radical written methods as he notes that many successful mental methods begin by changing the problem to something that is easier and then adjusting the answer. He identifies a 'transformation' in which the problem $311 - 214$ is solved mentally by first considering $314 - 214$ and then subtracting 3 from the answer. In the example above, the calculation $732 - 476$ could be undertaken by first subtracting 432 and then a further 44. In a similar manner, where a calculation such as $300 - 186$ is problematic using the column arrangement of the standard algorithm it is probably best solved using a counting-on strategy from 186. A neat 'trick' for using the algorithm that children enjoy is to change the problem from $300 - 186$ to $299 - 186$ and then to add 1 to the result. These types of adjustment result in easier calculations and reflect valid mathematical thinking.

## Using blocks to model a calculation

In the 1960s and 1970s, structured materials like Dienes blocks, consisting of 'tens' rods and 'unit' cubes, were widely used to 'model' the traditional algorithms for addition and subtraction. The initial setting up of, for example, 4 tens and 3 unit blocks together with 2 tens and 7 unit blocks for addition can be identified with the vertical written problem for $43 + 27$ (Figure 7.4).

Comparing the steps for addition and subtraction reveals the way that modelling with blocks need to be carefully 'orchestrated' and although the calculation $43 + 27$ and $43 - 27$ may look similar, the actions needed are quite different. Setting up the subtraction sum in the same way is not helpful where children identify subtraction with 'take away' because the two numbers that are represented by the blocks can only be compared. Lack of success in using these materials has led to a shift to more 'mental-calculation friendly' manipulatives (Thompson, 2001). Reporting on a research study of children's understanding of the way blocks can be used to model addition and subtraction, Hart (1989) claims that there is little connection as the blocks appear to give a model only for those who already understand the algorithm. 'Referring children to materials because they are having trouble ... is of little help unless one is sure that they have a workable method of setting up objects in order to mirror symbols.' She

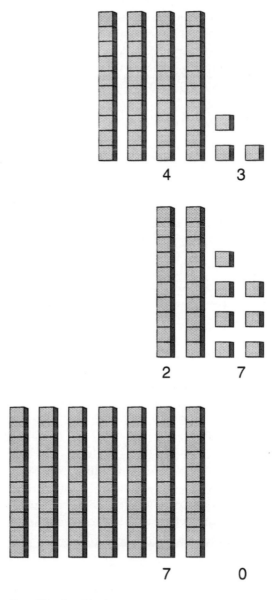

**Figure 7.4**   43 + 27 using blocks.

believes the gap between the two experiences is too large and children have great difficulty in making the connection. She showed that once children had been introduced to the written algorithm it was not long before they had completely forgotten any explanation and summarises the lack of connection between practical work and symbolic statements as 'Sums are Sums and Bricks are Bricks' (Hart, 1989).

## Introducing written methods for multiplication and division

Different contexts, particularly those that relate to the pupils' own experiences, are useful for generating multiplication and division problems, for example, costings for a class outing or cost per portion of different cereals. These will incorporate the important step of formulating the problem and identifying appropriate solution strategies, as well as interpreting the answer in a meaningful way. Collaboration on solving such problems may also generate comparisons between mental, written and calculator strategies and introduce the choices that pupils need to be able to make.

Motivation will be greater if the start for a calculation is a meaningful problem, such as 'If a person sleeps an average of 8 hours each night, how long does that person sleep in a year?' This multiplication of larger numbers involves 'breaking' the calculation into smaller parts. Repeated addition will become inefficient as the numbers get larger but this idea can be retained if pupils move progressively to more efficient 'chunks'. Doubling can also be a helpful strategy in the case of multiplication by 8 with jottings used to keep track of the subtotals that are found. There are many other ways this calculation may be done and partitioning using place value can be very effective. Written recording should express clearly the strategy used and children will need help to develop an organised format using mathematical symbols. A variety of approaches are illustrated for calculating $365 \times 8$ including 'messy working' that shows how the problem has been tackled.

| | |
|---|---|
| $300 \times 8 =$ 2400 | |
| $60 \times 8 =$ 480 | |
| $5 \times 8 =$ 40 | |
| $365 \times 8 =$ 2920 | |

$365 = 350 + 15$
$350 \times 8 = 700 \times 4$
$= 2800$
$15 \times 8 = 120$

365 doubled is 730
730 doubled is 1460
1460 doubled is 2920

$365 \times 8 = (400 \times 8) - (35 \times 8)$
$35 \times 8 = 35 \times 2 \times 4 = 280$
$400 \times 8 = 3200$
$3200 - 280 = 2920$

|  | 365 |
|---|---|
|  | $\times 8$ |
| $300 \times 8$ | 2400 |
| $60 \times 8$ | 480 |
| $5 \times 8$ | 40 |
|  | 2920 |

The 'rectangle' method is a good way to arrange a calculation based on place value as it emphasises the whole numbers rather than the digits:

| | 300 | 60 | 5 |
|---|---|---|---|
| 8 | 2400 | 480 | 40 |

The traditional 'long multiplication algorithm' is a highly efficient way to calculate but it has a very condensed form that makes it difficult to understand:

$$\begin{array}{r} 3\ 6\ 5 \\ \times 8 \\ \hline 2_2 9_5 2_4 0 \end{array}$$

Each time a multiplication of two digits gives a number greater than 9 (for example, $8 \times 5 = 40$), the 'tens part' must be 'carried forward' and added to the result of the next calculation (i.e. 4 must be added to the result of $8 \times 6 = 48$). The number to be 'carried forward' is usually written in small script in the column it will be added in and a considerable amount of working is done in the head. Because the contracted algorithm relies on steps that are not recorded it is important to keep expanded calculations as long as they are needed for sound understanding.

119

## Two-digit multipliers

The problem above could also be calculated in two parts by noting that 8 hours a night gives $8 \times 7 = 56$ hours sleep each week. Now the calculation for one year becomes $56 \times 52$ and the following recording methods relate to different approaches.

Different written methods for $56 \times 52$:

| With jottings | Using doubling and halving |
|---|---|
| $100 \times 56 = 5600$ | $52 \times 56 = 104 \times 28 = 208 \times 14 = 416 \times 7$ |
| $50 \times 56 = 2800$ | Now $400 \times 7 = 2800$ |
| $2 \times 56 = 112$ | $10 \times 7 = 70$ |
| so $52 \times 56 = 2800 + 112 = 2912$ | $6 \times 7 = 42$ |
| | and $2800 + 70 + 42 = 2912$ |

### Rectangle method

|  | 50 | 6 |
|---|---|---|
| 50 | 2500 | 300 |
| 2 | 100 | 12 |

so $56 \times 52 = 2500 + 300 + 100 + 12 = 2912$

### Gelosia method

The traditional algorithm may involve different stages, from an extended version that show all the stages in the calculation, to the contracted version where much of the working is done mentally:

| traditional extended | | 56 | | traditional |
|---|---|---|---|---|
| 56 | | $\times\ 52$ | | contracted |
| $\times\ 52$ | | 112 | $2 \times 56$ | 56 |
| 12 | $6 \times 2$ | 2500 | $50 \times 50$ | $\times 52$ |
| 100 | $50 \times 2$ | 300 | $50 \times 6$ | 112 |
| 300 | $6 \times 50$ | 2912 | $52 \times 56$ | 2800 |
| 2500 | $50 \times 50$ | | | 2912 |
| 2912 | | | | |

It is important that pupils retain flexibility in their approach so that they can use a method appropriate for the numbers involved. The problem 24 × 39, for example, can be tackled mentally if pupils can multiply 24 by 40. Sharing ways of thinking about calculations, and comparing ways to record working, will enable pupils to progress in their efficiency and develop understanding of the mathematical principles that underlie the different methods.

## Multiplying a three-digit number by a two-digit number

When multiplying a three-digit number by a two-digit number, for example in the problem 'How many hours are there in 1 year?', the different stages of the calculation need to be recorded in an organized way and a vertical arrangement can be appropriate. Some pupils will prefer to work with the whole numbers at all stages and some may use doubling and halving.

| With jottings | Using doubling and halving |
|---|---|
| 300 × 24 = 300 × 12 × 2 = 7200 | 365 × 24 = 730 × 12 |
| 60 × 24 = 60 × 12 × 2 = 1440 | 730 × 10 = 7300 |
| 5 × 24 = 120 | 730 × 2 = 1460 |
| 7200 + 1440 + 120 = 8760 | 730 × 12 = 8760 |
| 1 year is 8760 hours | 1 year is 8760 hours |

Rectangle method

|  | 300 | 60 | 5 |
|---|---|---|---|
| 20 | 6000 | 1200 | 100 |
| 4 | 1200 | 240 | 20 |

So 365 × 24 = 6000 + 1200 + 100 + 1200 + 240 + 20 = 8760 hours

| traditional | extended | | traditional |
|---|---|---|---|
| 365 | | | 365 |
| × 24 | | | × 24 |
| 6000 | 20 × 300 | 365 × 20 | 7300 |
| 1200 | 20 × 60 | 365 × 4 | 1460 |
| 120 | 24 × 5 | | 8760 |
| 240 | 4 × 60 | | |
| 1200 | 4 × 300 | | |
| 8760 | | | |

## Making connections

It is often easier to calculate the multiple of a number starting with facts that are already known. Starting with any number and repeatedly doubling gives 2 times, 4 times and 8 times that number. Multiplying by 10 may also be recorded as a known fact. From these, all other multiples can be derived by adding. The calculation for 26 × 17 may be recorded in stages:

$$1 \times 17 = 17$$
$$2 \times 17 = 34$$
$$4 \times 17 = 68$$
$$8 \times 17 = 136$$
$$10 \times 17 = 170$$

Now $26 \times 17 = (10 \times 17) + (10 \times 17) + (4 \times 17) + (2 \times 17) = 170 + 170 + 68 + 34 = 442$

Since the same multiples, 2, 4, 8 ... are used each time, a repertoire is developed of related facts about the way any number can be constructed from these powers of 2 (for example, 26 = 20 + 4 + 2).

## Division with larger numbers and a single digit divisor

Division problems can be interpreted in two ways relating to intuitive ideas of sharing or grouping. These ideas need to be reconciled with written recording, and informal jottings will help teachers to appreciate pupils' interpretation of problems. As noted in the last chapter, it can be helpful to identify division with repeated subtraction of 'chunks' and written recording can provide a structured record that will help children keep track. The calculation 96 ÷ 4, for example, involves 'chunking' the 96 into numbers that are associated with four and a written record may be made in horizontal or vertical format:

| | |
|---|---|
| $96 = 40 + 40 + 16$<br>$= (10 \times 4) + (10 \times 4) + (4 \times 4)$<br>$= 24 \times 4$ | $\begin{array}{rl} 96 & \\ -40 & \times\ 10 \\ \hline 56 & \\ -40 & \times\ 10 \\ \hline 16 & \\ -16 & \times\ 4 \\ \hline 0 & \times\ 24 \end{array}$ |

The traditional algorithm is a very compacted way to record a calculation but relies on precise first guesses and good understanding of the structure of a large number. Within the calculation, digits are used and children lose the values of the whole numbers. More long-winded recording allows pupils to reinforce their understanding of the process of repeated subtraction of chunks. For the traditional algorithm pupils will need to be taught that '4 divided into 9' gives the 'tens' part of the answer and the remainder of 1 becomes 10 units. This is a shorthand for '4 divided into 90 gives 20 with 10 remaining'.

| | |
|---|---|
| $\begin{array}{r} 2\ \ 4 \\ 4\overline{)9\,^{1}6} \end{array}$ | Alternatively,<br>$96 = 100 - 4$ and $100 = 25 \times 4$<br>allows this calculation to be done<br>mentally! |

If pupils follow rules without understanding, errors will occur as the digits become the focus instead of the whole values of the numbers and such a difficulty may arise when zeros need to be included in parts of the calculation and a common error occurs when they are omitted altogether:

$$\begin{array}{r} 2\ 9 \quad \text{rem 2} \\ 6\overline{)1^{1}25^{5}6} \end{array}$$

The following examples show some different written approaches for the calculation 1256 ÷ 6:

$$\begin{array}{r} 6\overline{)1256} \\ \underline{600 \times 100} \\ 656 \\ \underline{600 \times 100} \\ 56 \\ 54 \quad \times 9 \\ \text{Answer 209 rem 2} \end{array}$$

1256 = 1200 + 56
1200 = 200 × 6
56 = 9 × 6 rem 2

Answer 209 with 2 left

$$\begin{array}{r} 02\ 0\ 9 \quad \text{rem 2} \\ 6\overline{)1^{1}2\ 5^{5}6} \end{array}$$

## Division with two-digit divisors

For division by a two-digit divisor there are various methods and the main advantage of a strategy based more explicitly on repeated subtraction is that the *same* method can be extended to work with two-digit divisors. The step from the traditional short division algorithm to long division, however, needs a re-organization of the written recording to included additional working. Written recording is most easily understood if it relates to the children's way of thinking about the problem. In developing written recording to introduce better efficiency, children can be encouraged to discuss and compare their approaches and the ways they write them down.

Working with problems in 'real' contexts may suggest approaches that use doubling, halving or multiples of ten. In the example, '432 school children are going on an outing. If each bus takes 15 passengers, how many buses will be needed?' efficiency can be gained by using 'chunks' of 30 or 60 at a time:

|  | 432 |
|---|---:|
| 10 buses | −150 |
|  | 282 |
| 10 buses | −150 |
|  | 132 |
| 4 buses | −60 |
|  | 72 |
| 4 buses | −60 |
| Answer 28 remainder | 12 |
| add 1 more bus = 29 | |

Using 'chunking' to break 432 into numbers associated with 15
432 = 300 + 132
132 = 120 + 12

So 432 = 300 + 120 + 12
20 buses and 8 buses and 1 more

Where there is a context it is important to interpret the result as an answer to the problem rather than give a numerical solution. In the context above the answer '28 remainder 12' will not be appropriate as 29 buses will be needed.

The long division algorithm is a more condensed way to represent the calculation and many children understand better the chunking method above (Anghileri *et al.*, 2002; Anghileri, 2004).

$$
\begin{array}{r}
2\ 8 \quad \text{rem } 12 \\
15\overline{)4^43^{13}2} \\
3\ 0 \\
\hline
1\ 3\ 2 \\
1\ 2\ 0 \\
\hline
1\ 2
\end{array}
$$

First 15 is divided into 43 and this will give 2 as the tens part of the answer. The corresponding 30 (tens) is placed under the 43 of the 432. When 30 is subtracted from 43, the 13 gives the number of tens remaining. To this is 'joined' the 2 units to make 13 tens and 2 units, or 132. Now 15 is divided into 132, probably with some pencil and paper jottings, e.g. 15, 30, 60, 120 ... showing 8 × 15 is 120. This method can be very confusing for some children and is not necessary if the chunking method can be mastered.

This particular problem could also be solved mentally if the fact that 30 × 15 = 450 is known:

432 = 450 − 18
450 would need 30 buses
18 fewer so 29 buses are needed

For some calculations, initial re-organization into the formal algorithm will be of no help, for example, 'A farm shop sells about 72 eggs each day. How many days will 300 eggs take to sell?' In this example the traditional long division algorithm will result in precisely the same problem $300 \div 72$.

$$
\begin{array}{r}
0\ 0\ ? \\
72\overline{)3\ 0^{30}0}
\end{array}
$$

For problems like this it will be necessary to take a different approach or to use a calculator. Approaches based on repeated subtraction will work and the choice of appropriate chunks can make the calculation efficient:

|        |        |
|-------:|-------:|
|        | 300    |
| 1 day  | $-72$  |
|        | 228    |
| 2 days | $-144$ |
|        | 84     |
| 1 day  | $-72$  |
| 4 days rem | 12 |

|        |        |
|-------:|-------:|
|        | 300    |
| 4 days | $-288$ |
| 4 days rem | 12 |

## A postscript on algorithms

All pupils are expected ultimately to use *efficient* written methods for calculating but the only way such methods can be meaningful is if they are developed progressively to support and extend mental strategies (Anghileri, 2001a, 2004). Determining an appropriate strategy, whether it is mental, part-written, written or using a calculator, will depend on the problem itself, the numbers involved and the purpose of the calculation. Children will need to develop skills in selecting an appropriate method and DfEE advise that 'when faced with a calculation, no matter how large or how difficult the numbers may appear to be, encourage them first to ask themselves: "Can I do this in my head?"' But teachers will need to support children in recording their working, particularly as method marks are often given in national tests. There has been a move away from traditional algorithms and QCA reports frequently illustrate the pitfalls of children using algorithms

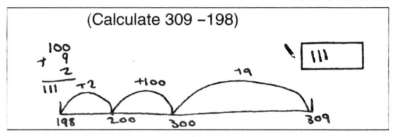

**Figure 7.5** Example of a self-drawn number line (QCA, 2003).

incorrectly while successfully using informal methods such as a 'self-drawn number line' (Figure 7.5).

The arguments for continuing to teach written algorithms are usually identified with their conciseness as written records, and the way they encapsulate rules and relationships among numbers in a formal procedure. Their 'elegance' and 'rigour' rather than their utilitarian nature can give them a valued position in mathematics learning provided the purpose in teaching them is made clear to the learners. Plunkett (1979), however, argues that 'the reasons for teaching the standard written algorithm are out of date and their utilisation leads to frustration, unhappiness and a deteriorating attitude to mathematics'.

By removing the emphasis on a standard approach it will be possible to focus on the many ways that any problem may be solved, and to focus on the relationships between numbers, and the operations for combining them, that will be the basis for successful problem-solving and more abstract algebraic thinking the pupils will use in later mathematics.

### Activities

1. Look at both the latest national tests for Key Stage 2 (calculator allowed and calculator not allowed) and identify all the calculations that need to be done. Identify good methods for doing each of these calculations and discuss your views with a peer.
2. Look at the report on these tests to see what methods are generally used by the pupils, and what advice is given by the National Assessment Agency.

127

# CHAPTER 8

# Teaching Approaches

The chapters of this book have aimed to explain how the foundations of number sense can be seen in the connections that show how numbers relate to each other within a logical structure and how new facts can be linked to those that are already known. This chapter will discuss teaching approaches that are most appropriate in developing children's number sense and will make reference to some of the research studies that are pertinent.

## Working with numbers in context

The traditional sequence of school activities, from easy numbers and their representation to complex numbers and calculations, does not take account of the way children learn. Just as language is developed by exposing children to a rich environment of words used in appropriate contexts, so number sense begins to develop when they are presented with opportunities to talk about *numbers wherever they occur*. Learning takes place whenever children reflect on what they are seeing and hearing and involvement in 'number conversations' can begin from the earliest age. Personal experiences (for example, four sweets – and eat one makes three!, the number 35 bus, a second chance, 20p for the hair dryer at the swimming pool) are starting points that should not be ignored. If children are exposed to numbers in this way, numbers will have meaning within a real context and children will use them confidently, identifying mathematics as a powerful tool for making sense of the world.

Numbers need to be presented in a realistic setting in order to make sense to young children. However, they can and should also be presented orally, as linguistic entities in their own right. To be able to count 'one hundred, two hundred, three hundred ...' does not indicate that these numbers are understood but the fascination of 'inventing' such large numbers reinforces a pattern that is generalizable and fundamental in the number system. As the chapters of this book have shown, counting is a key skill for understanding numbers. Aubrey (1997) reports that on entry to schooling 'the children with highest rote counting scores tended to have consistently high scores across [a range of] number tasks' including counting backwards and simple number operations. She notes that 'teachers' intuitive knowledge about children and teaching may *not* be well-connected' (original italics) to what children are already capable of and proposes that teaching needs to focus on 'fine-grain analysis of the way teaching and learning interact' in order to develop most effectively children's existing number sense (Aubrey, 1997, p. 29). Research evidence also suggests that very young children are capable of handling larger numbers in more complex ways than teachers have conventionally believed or assumed (Munn, 1994; Merttens, 1996; Thompson, 1997).

Whitebread (1999) advocates the approach to teaching which he calls 'emergent mathematics' in parallel with ideas of 'emergent writing'. It is based on the theory that children need to develop their understanding of numbers by playing with them and using them for their own purposes. In such an approach, children are invited to talk about their mathematical ideas with other children and with the teacher. They are encouraged to focus on mathematical processes and represent them in a way that makes sense to them, so becoming aware of their own and other peoples' thinking. By presenting real problems to be tackled in a meaningful context it will not always be appropriate to limit the numbers involved but this will give a better impression of the ways that mathematics is relevant to their lives than abstract activities from schemes or texts. By involving children in the sorts of activities that reflect everyday use of numbers they become aware of *how* numbers are used and also *why* they are used. As a result they develop the motivation to master for themselves the many skills and connections that explain number work.

In an 'emergent' approach children are encouraged 'to make their own representations of mathematical problems, processes and procedures before they are introduced to the conventional symbols' because the emphasis is on developing confidence in their own thinking (Whitebread, 1999, p. 31). Although children may well notice conventional symbols from an early age (for example, '+' and '−' on video controls) they need to take the initiative in using them when *they* think these are appropriate to express *their* ideas and findings. Children's own representations give clues about how they are working things out and this 'enables teachers to assess and build on children's thinking and prevents the inappropriate imposition of images on their thinking' (Gifford, 1997, p. 86). Traditional sums presented as written tasks can limit children's experiences where symbols such as '+', '−' and '=' are given narrow meanings and this can lead to inflexible use of such symbols. By sharing their own ideas about the way calculations can be recorded, under the guidance of a teacher, young children can be exposed to a great many ways of writing mathematics while retaining ownership of their personal ideas.

Meta-cognitive awareness and control are also identified as important features of emergent mathematics: not only do children develop strategies, they also develop the ability to use them appropriately (Whitebread, 1999). This ability to consider different possible procedures is called 'meta-cognitive' since the *procedures* occur at the cognitive 'level' while *reflecting on them* occurs at a higher 'level' of awareness. Knowing that adding 19 is best achieved by adding 20 and subtracting 1, while adding 12 is best achieved by adding 10 and then 2 more, are examples of where meta-cognitive awareness will result in different procedures for adding according to the numbers involved. Although children may learn some standard procedures, using number sense involves departure from these methods where the numbers warrant a different approach.

## Building on what children know when they start school

Some children have difficulty relating the number work they encounter on entering school with the use of numbers they have experienced outside school. Aubrey (1997) discusses the 'gap between children's own informal, invented number knowledge and the formal requirements of the reception class curriculum'. She reports that in a research project attempting to shed light on typical early-years practice it became clear that this 'does not match the range and diversity of knowledge, skills and strategies in a variety of number, counting and arithmetic tasks for children entering school'. In the first, and more so in the second year of schooling, schemes and worksheets were thought 'to offer a framework for planning the introduction of sorting, matching and ordering numbers' that did not reflect the stage of children's understanding or take account of children's informal knowledge. Inappropriate emphasis was placed on 'practical colour, pattern and shape recognition, matching, sorting and ordering of shape, comparison and ordering of quantity, counting and recording and comparison of sets'. 'Children did not appear to relate their in-school activities with structured materials to their out-of-school, context specific problem-solving' (Aubrey, 1997, p. 23). Findings of the research suggest that teachers' intuitive knowledge about what activities are appropriate for consolidating or extending the understanding of their pupils can be better informed by analysis of the children's existing knowledge. Research shows that 'pupils learn more when their teachers know their attainment and can act on this information' (Askew and Wiliam, 1995, p. 20).

To help children transfer their informal knowledge of numbers to practical applications of this knowledge in the classroom, activities can be devised to reflect situations outside school where numbers have been seen and used. Role play areas in the classroom such as a café or pet shop present opportunities for children to recognize numerals and use the language of numbers. Activities such as making price tags or organizing money in a cash box give realistic purposes for number work and can generate discussion through which formal language and symbols may be introduced. Working together – beginning to record and to share ideas – will be an important way to develop skills in mathematical thinking and to establish methods for communicating this thinking through words, pictures and symbols.

Diversity in children's mastery of number facts can make it difficult for the teacher as the number work of individual children will progress at different rates that need to be monitored but cannot be predicted. Until they enter school, learning has taken place within the child's family and the wider community, through involvement in talking and thinking about issues that have arisen. Much of the children's learning will continue to be developed outside the classroom and a partnership between school and home will be needed to establish common goals and learning objectives that are shared with parents and carers (Merttens and Vass, 1993).

## Teachers as listeners

A key characteristic of early learning in the home is the opportunity for conversations in which the child, as the learner, often takes the initiative in asking the questions. Although this is not always possible in the classroom, an environment where children are encouraged to express their thinking and ask questions as well as answer them will encourage independent approaches to problem-solving. Children will need opportunities to talk about their own strategies and to discuss those used by others. Whether working orally or with written problems, it is important to listen to the explanations of individual children in order to ascertain their grasp of particular relationships and their ability to apply number sense rather than doggedly replicating a learned procedure (Anghileri, 1995a). The following examples illustrate responses that show a range of strategies for addition that were given by a child to explain the answers to mental calculations:

| | |
|---|---|
| [5 + 2 = 7] | '5, 6, 7 |
| [2 + 2 = 4] | 'because I know 2 and 2' |
| [3 + 4 = 7] | '3 and 3 is 6 and one more is 7' |
| [5 + 4 = 9] | 'because it is one less than 10' |

Each of these explanations refers to a different procedure for solving the addition problems and the variations show the way in which children can develop flexibility by selecting the most appropriate procedure for each problem. As they meet problems in a variety of contexts children will often respond more readily if the numerical calculations have some explicit meaning for themselves (for example, 'You are 5 years old and Stephen is 7. How much older is Stephen?'). Although the ultimate aim is for instant recall of basic number facts, such as the pairs that make 10 and other combinations such as 25 + 25, the strategies children develop on the way to knowing these facts will form the basis for calculation with larger numbers. Research results show that 'knowing by heart' and 'figuring out' support each other in children's learning about numbers (Askew and Wiliam, 1995, p. 8).

In developing mental calculating strategies, teachers need to pay careful attention to children's actions and words so that they may appreciate the subtle differences that exist (Anghileri, 1995a). This will help them to identify those who have achieved efficiency in their approaches and those who are persisting with more naïve and inefficient strategies. Children can learn to choose the calculation method with fewest steps (for example 11 − 3 would be calculated by counting back, while 11 − 8 would be calculated by counting on) but presenting appropriate examples can help to clarify the benefits of different approaches. More extreme examples (such as 34 − 5 and 34 − 28) can be introduced to stimulate discussion about effective approaches.

There can be difficulties for teachers where much of the calculating is done orally and little written recording takes place. Brown (1997) reports that although she encourages mental mathematics in her classroom, she admits finding it problematic with respect to 'assessment and some kind of monitoring of progress'. Where there are no written records of the mental strategy children are using, discussion becomes even more important as a way to monitor the children's thinking. Recording some of the ideas will be necessary for clear communication and this can be the focus of follow-up work, rather than the driving force in the calculating process. There may be some scepticism from the public at large in placing the emphasis on mental mathematics rather than written recording, as there often is whenever traditions are challenged. Teachers will need to use the available research and survey evidence to help persuade parents that delaying written calculating methods is educationally sound.

## Teaching number work as a social activity

Talking is a powerful tool as children continue to learn by listening and joining in conversations, using their logic and developing their language to match different situations. Mathematical learning will be dependent on the children being ready to reflect on the results of their thinking and make the transition to discuss results themselves. The classroom practice of children sharing in the learning process is sometimes referred to as *collective reflection* and identified with the *socio-norms* of the classroom through which children learn what is universally accepted and acceptable (Cobb *et al.*, 1997). Researchers have found it helpful to use the notions of *reflective discourse* to describe the classroom talk through which mathematical activity itself is objectified and becomes an explicit topic of conversation. The teacher's role is to guide and initiate shifts in this discourse so that what was previously done in action becomes an explicit topic of conversation.

Cobb *et al.* (1997) use an anecdote to explain the development of mathematical thinking that is possible under teacher guidance. Starting with visual images of 5 monkeys in 2 trees the children proceed working mentally, or with their fingers as 'perceptual substitutes', and propose different ways the monkeys could be distributed:

| | |
|---|---|
| Anna: | I think that three could be in the little tree and two could be in the big tree. |
| Teacher: | OK, three could be in the little tree and two could be in the big tree [writes 3\|2 between the trees]. So, still 3 and 2 but they are in different trees this time; three in the little one and two in the big one. Linda you have another way? |
| Linda: | Five could be in the big one. |
| Teacher: | OK, five could be in the big one [writes 5] and then how many would be in the little one? |
| Linda: | Zero. |

Here the teacher gives a commentary from the perspective of one who could judge which aspects of the children's activity might be mathematically significant within what the researchers refer to as *mathematizing discourse*.

The teacher later asks: 'Is there a way that we could be sure and know we've gotten all the ways?'

Now the results of the activity become explicit objects of the discussion that can be related to each other. The discourse shifts from generating the possible ways, to operating on the results of that generative activity – this could lead to a systematic ordering of results and strategies for testing if the list is complete. Cobb *et al.* conclude that 'it is this feature of the episode that leads us to classify it as an example of *reflective discourse*' and conclude that 'children's participation in this type of discourse *constitutes conditions for the possibility of mathematical learning*' (Cobb et al., 1997, p. 212).

## Identifying and working with misconceptions

Although it is tempting in a class discussion to invite children whose responses are correct to talk about the way they tackled a solution, it is important to create an environment that accepts every child's thinking as equally valid. Asking a child 'how did you arrive at that answer?' when the answer is incorrect will sometimes lead to individuals reviewing their procedures and correcting themselves, but may also lead to opportunities for other children to help put right any erroneous ideas. Rather than 'spreading' misconceptions through sharing them, children will learn to reason about their strategies and follow the reasoning of others, thus developing important skills in communication of mathematical thinking. Askew and Wiliam (1995) cite research evidence that supports the idea that learning is more effective when common misconceptions are addressed, exposed and discussed in teaching. 'We have to accept that pupils will make some generalizations that are not correct and many of these misconceptions remain hidden unless the teacher makes specific efforts to uncover them.'

Many children will have misconceptions and make wrong generalizations at some stage in their mathematical learning. In an effort to find more efficient ways of working, able pupils will sometimes try to apply rules that they know in new situations or make wrong generalizations. The counting sequence 29 followed by 20-10, for example, shows a child's sound strategy that does not apply in this particular situation. Verbalizing such thinking will not only help the child involved but all children can benefit by 'seeing' how other people are thinking about numbers.

Watching and listening to children is also important for detecting errors and misconceptions. In the example '11 − 3', the number eleven is sometimes included within the three to be counted (11, 10, 9) and the wrong answer '9' is given. It is important to identify such misconceptions early and work again with concrete materials or imagined contexts ('If I start with 11 buttons in a row and cover up three, how many will I still see?'). Encouraging children to use their fingers and count out loud will give opportunities to assess their strategies. In his 'alternative approach' to the number curriculum, Thompson (1997) proposes that one of the actions to be incorporated into classroom teaching is 'to legitimate and encourage the use of fingers and counting procedures' particularly for simple addition and subtraction.

## Characterizing effective teaching approaches

The previous sections suggest that classroom talk is an essential element of effective teaching and this section will go on to look at a study that has attempted to characterise the most effective teaching approaches for mathematics in primary school. In a study of effective numeracy teaching, Askew *et al.* (1997) use the term *connectionist* to describe approaches where emphasis is given to the links between different ideas in mathematics and to encouraging pupils to draw on their mathematical understanding to develop their own strategies in problem-solving. By gathering evidence from a sample of 90 teachers, the researchers found out what teachers believed, knew, understood and did. The study gained data on resulting outcomes in terms of pupil learning gains for over 2000 pupils. In this study the researchers found that highly effective teachers believe that pupils develop strategies and networks of ideas by being challenged to think, through explaining, listening and problem-solving, and use teaching approaches that build on pupils' own mental strategies with teacher intervention to make these more efficient. This teacher intervention appears to be crucial in developing children's ideas in a progressive way.

A different category of teaching approach identified in this study is that of the '*discovery*'-orientated teacher who tended to treat all methods of calculation as equally acceptable. This approach focused on encouraging pupils' creation of their own methods and was based on building their confidence and ability in practical methods. These teachers' primary belief was that 'becoming numerate is an individual activity derived from actions on objects'. Such teachers also believe that pupils' own strategies are the most important and that pupil misunderstandings are 'the result of pupils not being "ready" to learn the ideas'. This contrasts with the connectionist orientation view that 'pupils' misunderstandings need to be recognized, made explicit and worked on' with pupils being 'challenged and struggling to overcome difficulties'.

A third category was identified as those teachers who believed in the importance of their pupils acquiring a collection of procedures or routines, particularly in regard to pencil and paper methods. These were characterized as having a '*transmission*' orientation encompassing the view that teaching is most effective through verbal explanations of routines and results in the use of 'track laying' – the use of pencil and paper methods with styles of recording in advance of when they may be appropriate. As an example of this 'track laying', in traditional texts pupils may be introduced to the 'bus shelter' notation for division $4\overline{)36}$ at a stage when the problem may be solved by recall. Encouragement is given to use this written algorithmic format which sets out the problems in vertical format $4\overline{)36}$, and places emphasis on the arrangement where the answer '9 is placed above the 6' (Nuffield 4, *Teacher's Handbook*, 1992). The written recording does not facilitate the calculation but prepares the format that may be used for later, more complex, calculations. Where this is not clear to the children, confusion may arise about the methods they should use to solve the calculation itself.

In this research study, the 'transmission teachers', who gave priority to pupils acquiring a collection of standard arithmetical methods over establishing understanding and connections, produced lower numeracy gains when the children were tested towards the beginning and again towards the end of a school year. Lower numeracy gains were also associated with the 'discovery' approach which gave priority to the use of practical equipment, and delayed the introduction of more abstract ideas 'until [the teacher] felt a child was ready for them'. In the most successful 'connectionist' approach, teachers believed that *being numerate* requires having an rich network of connections between different mathematical ideas and being able to select and use a range of strategies (Askew *et al.* (1997)).

## Teaching mental strategies

Although there has been a long tradition in *mental recall* and children have, for generations, been required to commit to memory a
variety of mathematical facts and formulae, early introduction of
standard written algorithms has meant that *mental strategies* have
not been explicitly taught in the classroom. The progressive development reflected in most schemes and texts has involved stages
towards the standard methods to be reproduced and practised in
written exercises. In teaching these standard written approaches
the expectation has been that children will have an efficient procedure for calculating that they can apply to any number problem.
The reality has been that the curtailed written record of a procedure based on manipulating digits, rather than a holistic approach
to the numbers involved, has made it difficult (or impossible) to
understand, and arithmetic for many children has in the past been
reduced to the application of rules. Researchers have shown that
the gap between a child's way of thinking about a problem and the
formal procedure of an algorithm has presented difficulties that
could be avoided with a more progressive approach to gaining
efficiency, and more flexibility through written presentation based
on mental strategies (Thompson, 1997; Anghileri and Beishuizen,
1998; Anghileri *et al.*, 2002).

The teaching of mental calculations has for some time been the
focus of research in the Netherlands and van den Heuvel-
Panhuizen (2001) identifies ways in which the Dutch curriculum
has been developed to support mental strategies. It is the Realistic
Mathematics Education (RME) approach to first engage with the
children's informal strategies, elaborating on them later, and then
move towards more formal standard procedures. This is considered to be a much better learning activity than the other way
round. Rather than beginning with certain abstractions or definitions to be applied later, teaching starts with rich contexts demanding mathematical organization or, in other words, 'contexts
that can be mathematized'. Structured materials such as a 100-
bead string and an empty number line are introduced system-
atically to support mental methods and then written calculations
are built progressively from the children's intuitive approaches.

Research has shown the effectiveness of such practices in the

Netherlands compared with more traditional teaching in the UK (Anghileri and Beishuizen, 1998; Anghileri, 2004; Anghileri *et al.*, 2002). A characterization of different teaching approaches in the Netherlands and the UK identifies the benefits of written methods that are more compatible with the sense that children make of different problems (Beishuizen and Anghileri, 1998). 'It is true that, in the beginning, non-standard methods can be time-consuming; but if the learners are allowed to develop them further, they become curtailed and more efficient' (Beishuizen, 1997). Where similar teaching approaches have been implemented in the UK, there have been reports on the positive responses that teachers have made to the change of focus from written to mental strategies. Keith Holloway (1997) describes the findings of a group of primary teachers who explored the issues surrounding mental strategies in school. These teachers found that written versions of children's mental strategies show little similarity to standard algorithms and that they are based on different understanding of number. Positive responses to mental mathematics were observed amongst the children with a rise in self-esteem of a number of individuals as debates spontaneously occurred where children tried to help others understand their ways of doing things, and as they discussed which ways are more efficient. Instead of removing difficulties teacher were more likely to pose problems that addressed misconceptions directly and to encourage children to think divergently with open questions. Teachers reported that 'children have felt freer to express themselves in a confident and accurate way because the format has not been questioning'.

## Using calculators to motivate and empower children

In addition to research projects such as those discussed above, there has been a notable curriculum development project in the UK that has influenced ways to develop children's confidence and initiative in working with numbers. The PrIME (Primary Initiatives in Mathematics Education) project (Shuard *et al.*, 1991), with its integrated CAN (Calculator Aware Number) project has had widespread influence on teachers, and the impact of these projects has been recognised around the world (Ruthven, 2001). In the innovative approaches introduced in these projects, it was the fundamental policy that no algorithms were taught but that children were encouraged to devise, and to share, their own ways of calculating with a strong emphasis on mental calculations. Teachers did not spend time showing, or trying to show children how to do calculations, but devised tasks that were rich in numerical connections. The emphasis was on creativity as children gained confidence in their own ideas and even began to devise their own mathematical tasks, and this very much involved pattern-spotting.

Likening it to the 'creativity and independence more usually experienced in an art class', Rousham (1999) reports the 'enjoyment and changed attitude' to mathematics as children in the project schools wanted to 'do maths for the pleasure of exploring numbers'. The removal of standard procedures for calculating enabled children to try out their own ideas, while correct calculations on the calculator formed the basis for identifying patterns and developing awareness of relationships among numbers and between operations. In his discussion of calculators as a cognitive learning tool in the classroom, Rousham refers to the way six- and seven-year-olds tackled missing number problems such as $\Diamond + \square = 28$. He uses the term 'feedback loop' for the dialogue of question and response that children can have with a calculator. He suggests that the machine not only answers silently and reliably every question, but gives a 'fresh and unasked-for piece of information' that can guide further questioning. This environment may be helpful in preventing children from developing misconceptions. The feedback loop goes beyond a 'trial and improve' method because children become interested in the transient displays in a long calculation and Rousham (1999) reports children sitting and thinking about what is displayed in a manner that is not typical of adults.

Rousham does, however, warn that 'children need real access over some considerable time to become sufficiently familiar and confident with [calculators] to cross that "threshold" of familiarity which allows them to use the calculator's power for the kind of high order exploration of tasks' which he noticed during the CAN project.

There was little in the way of formal research evaluation at the time of the PrIME and CAN projects but many anecdotal reports exist that report the effectiveness of the innovative teaching approaches. Subsequent research studies in schools involved with the project have been undertaken (Ruthven, 2001). In an evaluation involving 'post-CAN' schools, that were previously involved with the project, Ruthven (1998) reports that pupils 'were encouraged to develop informal methods of calculation and to use calculators to explore number and execute demanding computations'. He noted that investigative and problem-solving activities formed an important part of the curriculum and it was here that calculators were most likely to be used. When compared with pupils in schools where calculators were less readily available and 'the sense was more of working towards written methods', he reports that 'while there was acknowledgement of pupils' informal strategies in the non-project schools, there was less emphasis on developing and refining them, and more on adopting approved written methods, predominantly standard column methods'.

In the project schools, pupils had been 'explicitly taught mental methods based on "smashing up" or "breaking down" numbers' and were 'expected to behave responsibly in regulating their use of calculators to complement their mental methods'. In contrast, in the non-project schools, 'daily experience of "quickfire calculation" had offered pupils a model of mental calculation as something to be done quickly or abandoned'. Calculator use provided opportunities for reflection on the output in what Ruthven termed an *observe-predict-surpass* sequence, or a *diagnose-explain-reinforce* sequence. Rather than inhibiting pupils' ability to work with mental calculations, Ruthven found that when tested on standard calculations, the pupils from a 'calculator-aware' environment were more inclined to use mental computation than written column methods or multiple use of a calculator, and were 'less prone to fall back on the use of written or calculator methods'. Additionally, in his conclusions he note that effective use of the calculator enable pupils to tackle problems which call for computation 'beyond their current capabilities'. Rather than reducing mathematical understanding, attention is turned to the underlying mathematical ideas associated with a calculation (Ruthven, 1999).

## Towards a new generation of mathematical thinkers

It will be evident in children's approaches to problem-solving whether they are making their own sense of problems or simply trying to reproduce taught procedures. When children have confidence in tackling problems they may go beyond minimal requirements in calculating to produce an enhanced solution such as the second one in Figure 8.1.

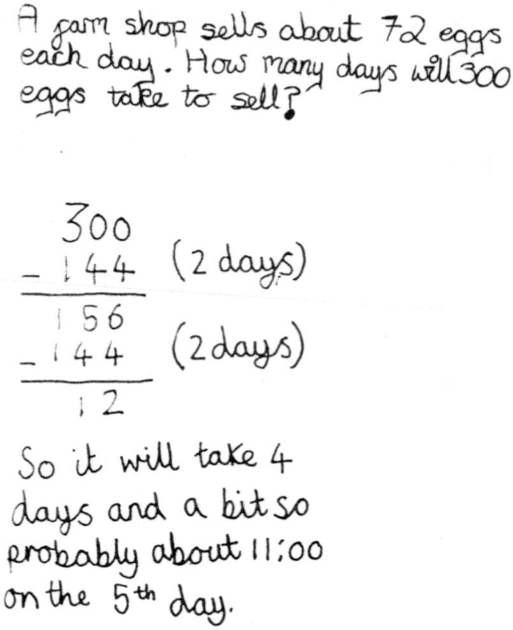

A farm shop sells about 72 eggs each day. How many days will 300 eggs take to sell?

$$
\begin{array}{r}
300 \\
-144 \quad (2\ days) \\
\hline
156 \\
-144 \quad (2\ days) \\
\hline
12
\end{array}
$$

So it will take 4 days and a bit so probably about 11:00 on the 5th day.

**Figure 8.1**   Number sense in problem-solving.

This solution shows a real *feel* for numbers that typifies what can be achieved when teaching is focused on developing children's *number sense*.

When arithmetic is taught as a logical structure of connected processes and results, rather than a sequence of standard procedures, children will learn that there is flexibility and choice in solving problems. As a result, they will develop *ownership* in making decisions and deriving meanings from their actions. It is this ownership that will help them to develop the confidence in their thinking and an *inclination* to work with numbers. If teaching approaches change so that children learn *connections* then the outcome could be a new generation of mathematical thinkers who will be autonomous learners driven on by their fascination with numbers.

## Activities

1. Take time to listen to an individual child explaining how they undertook a calculation. Focus on the *exact* words and the *meaning* these words have for the child.
2. Identify examples where children are using number sense rather than taught procedures. Suggest some tasks where there are better opportunities for children to use number sense.

# References

Anghileri, J (1995a) 'Language, arithmetic and the negotiation of meaning', *For the Learning of Mathematics*, **21** (3), 10–14.

Anghileri, J (1995b) 'Children's finger methods for multiplication', in *Mathematics in School*, **24** (1), 40–2.

Anghileri, J (1997) 'Uses of counting in multiplication and division', in I Thompson (ed.) *Teaching and Learning Early Number*. Buckingham: Open University Press.

Anghileri, J (1998) 'A discussion of different approaches to arithmetic teaching', in A. Olivier and K. Newstead (eds) *Proceedings of the Twenty-second International Conference for the Psychology of Mathematics Education*, **2**, 2–17.

Anghileri, J (1999) *Children's Mathematical Thinking in the Primary Year*. London: Continuum.

Anghileri, J (2000) 'Development of Division Strategies for Year 5 Pupils in Ten English Schools', in *British Education Research Journal*, **27** (1), 85–103.

Anghileri, J (2001a) 'Intuitive approaches, mental strategies and standard algorithms', in J Anghileri (ed.) *Principles and Practices in Arithmetic Teaching*. Buckingham: Open University Press.

Anghileri, J (2001b) 'What are we trying to achieve in teaching standard calculating procedures?', in M van den Heuvel-Panhuizen (ed.) *Proceedings of the 25th Conference of the International Group for the Psychology of Mathematics Education*, **2**, 41–8. Utrecht: PME.

Anghileri, J (2004) 'Disciplined calculators or flexible problem solvers?', in M J Høines and A B Fuglestad (eds) *Proceedings of the 28th Conference of the International Group for the Psychology of Mathematics Education*, **2**, 41–6. Bergen: PME.

Anghileri, J and Beishuizen, M (1998) 'Counting, chunking and the division algorithm', *Mathematics in School*, **27** (1), 2–4.

Anghileri, J, Beishuizen, M and Putten, C (2002) 'From informal strategies to structured procedures: mind the gap!', in *Educational Studies in Mathematics*, **49** (2), 149–70.

Askew, M, Brown, M, Rhodes, V, Wiliam, D, and Johnson, D (1997) *Effective Teachers of Numeracy: Report of a study carried out for the Teacher Training Agency*. London: King's College, London.

Askew, M and Wiliam, D (1995) *Recent Research in Mathematics Education 5–16*. London: HMSO.

Aubrey, C (1997) 'Children's early learning of number in school and out', in I Thompson (ed.) *Teaching and Learning Early Number*. Buckingham: Open University Press.

Australian Education Council (1991) *A National Statement on Mathematics for Australian Schools*. Carlton: Curriculum Corporation.

Beishuizen, M (1995) 'New Research into mental arithmetic strategies with two-digit numbers up to 100'. European Conference on Educational Research, University of Bath, September 1995.

Beishuizen, M (1997) 'Mental arithmetic: mental recall or mental strategies?', in *Mathematics Teaching*, **160**, 16–19.

Beishuizen, M (1999) 'The empty number line as a new model', in I Thompson (ed.) *Issues In Teaching Numeracy In Primary Schools*. Buckingham: Open University Press.

Beishuizen, M and Anghileri, J (1998) 'Which mental strategies in the early number curriculum? A comparison of British ideas and Dutch views', in *British Education Research Journal*, **25** (5), 519–38.

Brown, E (1997) 'Effective exercise in the mathematics classroom', in *Mathematics Teaching*, **160**, 12–15.

Brown, J and Van Lehn, K (1980) 'Repair theory: a generative theory of bugs in procedural skills', in *Cognitive Science* (4) 379–426.

Brown, M (1981) 'Number operations', in K Hart (ed.) *Children's Understanding of Mathematics: 11–16*. London: Murray.

Brown, M (2001) 'Influences on the teaching of number in England', in J Anghileri (ed.) *Principles and Practices in Arithmetic Teaching*. Buckingham: Open University Press.

Buys, K (2001) 'Progressive mathematization: sketch of a learning strand', in J Anghileri (ed.) *Principles and Practices in Arithmetic Teaching*. Buckingham: Open University Press.

Carpenter, T, Ansell, E, Franke, M, Fennema, E and Weisbeck, L (1993) 'Models of problem solving: A study of kindergarten children's problem-solving processes', in *Journal for Research in Mathematics Education*, **24**, 428–41.

Carpenter, T and Moser, J (1983) 'The acquisition of addition and subtraction concepts', in R Lesh and M Landau (eds) *The Acquisition of Mathematics Concepts and Processes*. New York: Academic Press.

Clarke, F and Kamii, C (1996) 'Identification of multiplicative thinking in children in grades 1–5', in *Journal for Research in Mathematics Education*, **27** (1), 41–51.

Cobb, P, Boufi, A, McClain, K and Whitenack, J (1997) 'Reflective discourse and collective reflection', in *Journal for Research in Mathematics Education*, **28** (3), 258–77.

Cockcroft, W (1982) *Mathematics Counts: Inquiry into the teaching of mathematics in schools.* London: HMSO.

Department for Education and Employment (1998) *The Implementation of the National Numeracy Strategy: Final report of the numeracy task force.* London: DfEE.

Department for Education and Employment (1999) *The National Numeracy Strategy Framework for Teaching Mathematics from Reception to Year 6.* London: DfEE.

Department for Education and Employment (2001) *The National Numeracy Strategy Framework for Teaching Mathematics: Years 7, 8 and 9.* London: DfEE.

Dickson, L, Brown, M and Gibson, O (1984) *Mathematics Teachers and Children: A teacher's guide to recent research.* London: Cassell.

Faux, G (1998) 'For the classroom – Gattegno charts', in *Mathematics Teaching*, **163**.

Fischbein, E, Deri, M, Nello, M and Marino, M (1985) 'The role of implicit models in solving verbal problems in multiplication and division', in *Journal for Research in Mathematics Education*, **16**, 3–17.

Fuson, K (1988) *Children's Counting And Concepts Of Number.* New York: Springer Verlag.

Fuson, K (1992) 'Research on whole number addition and subtraction', in D Grouws (ed.) *Handbook of research on mathematics teaching and learning*, 243–75. New York: Macmillan.

Fuson, K, Wearne, D, Hiebert, J, Murray, H, Human, P, Olivier, A, Carpenter, T and Fennema, E (1997) 'Children's conceptual structures for multidigit numbers and methods of multidigit addition and subtraction', in *Journal for Research in Mathematics Education*, **28** (2), 130–62.

Gelman, R and Gallistel, C (1978) *The Child's Understanding Of Number.* Cambridge: Harvard University Press.

Gifford, S (1997) '"When should they start doing sums?" A critical consideration of the "emergent mathematics" approach', in I Thompson (ed.) *Teaching And Learning Early Number.* Buckingham: Open University Press.

Ginsburg, H (1977) *Children's Arithmetic: The Learning Process.* New York: Van Nostrand.

Gray, E and Tall, D (1994) 'Duality, ambiguity, and flexibility: a "proceptual" view of simple arithmetic', in *Journal for Research in Mathematics Education*, **25**, 116–40.

Greer, B (1992) 'Multiplication and division as models of situations', in D

Grouws (ed.) *Handbook of Research on Mathematics Teaching and Learning*, 276–95. New York: Macmillan.

Hart, K (1989) 'There is little connection', in P Ernest (ed.) *Mathematics Teaching: The state of the art.* Lewes: The Falmer Press.

Hatch, G (1998) 'Replace your mental arithmetic test with a game', in *Mathematics in School*, **27** (1), 32–5.

Holloway, K (1997) 'Exploring mental maths', in *Mathematics Teaching,* **160**, 26–9.

Huckstep, P (1999) 'How can mathematics be useful?', in *Mathematics in School*, **28** (2), 15–17.

Hughes, M (1986) *Children and Number.* Oxford: Blackwell.

Kouba, VL and Franklin, K (1995) 'Multiplication and Division: Sense making and meaning', in *Teaching Children Mathematics*, **1** (9), 574–7.

McIntosh, A, Reys, B and Reys, R (1992) 'A proposed framework for examining number sense', in *For the Learning of Mathematics*, **12** (3), 25–31.

Menne, J (2001) 'Jumping ahead: An innovative teaching programme', in J Anghileri (ed.) *Principles and Practices in Arithmetic Teaching.* Buckingham: Open University Press.

Merttens, R (1996) *Teaching Numeracy: Mathematics in the Primary Classroom.* Leamington Spa: Scholastic.

Merttens, R and Vass, J (eds) (1993) *Partnership in Maths: Parents and Schools: the IMPACT Project.* London: Falmer.

Moss, J and Case, R (1999) 'Developing Children's Understanding of the Rational Numbers: A New Model and an Experimental Curriculum', in *Journal for Research in Mathematics Education*, **30** (2), 122–47.

Mulligan, J and Mitchelmore, M (1997) 'Young children's intuitive models of multiplication and division', in *Journal for Research in Mathematics Education*, **28** (3), 309–30.

Munn, P (1994) 'The early development of literacy and numeracy skills', in *European Early Childhood Research Journal*, **2** (1), 5–18.

Munn, P (1997) 'Children's beliefs about counting', in I Thompson (ed) *Teaching and Learning Early Numbers.* Buckingham: Open University Press.

Murray, H, Olivier, A and Human, P (1991) 'Young children's division strategies', in F Furinghetti (ed.) *Proceedings of the Fifteenth International Conference for the Psychology of Mathematics Education*, **3**, 49–56.

National Council for Teachers of Mathematics (2000) *Principles and Standards for School Mathematics.* Reston: NCTM.

Nuffield 4 (1991) *Teacher's Handbook.* Harlow: Longman.

Nunes, T and Bryant, P (1996) *Children Doing Mathematics.* Oxford: Blackwell Publishers.

# References

Nunes, T, Schlieman, A and Caraher, D (1993) *Street Mathematics and School Mathematics*. New York: Cambridge University Press.

Parr, A (1994) 'Games for Playing', in *Mathematics in School*, **23** (3), 29–30.

Pepper, KL and Hunting, RP (1998) 'Preschoolers' counting and sharing', in *Journal for Research in Mathematics Education*, **29**, 164–83.

Piaget, J (1965) *The Child's Concept Of Number*. New York: Norton.

Plunkett, S (1979) 'Decompositon and all that rot', in *Mathematics in School*, **8** (3), 2–7.

Qualifications and Curriculum Authority (1999) *Teaching Mental Calculation Strategies*. London: QCA.

Qualifications and Curriculum Authority (2003) *Standards at Key Stage 2 English, Mathematics and Science: A report for headteachers, class teachers and assessment coordinators on the 2003 national curriculum assessments*. London: QCA.

Rousham, L (1999) 'CAN calculators make a difference?', in J Anghileri (ed.) *Children's Mathematical Thinking in the Primary Years*. London: Continuum.

Ruthven, K (1998) 'The use of mental, written and calculator strategies of numerical computation by upper-primary pupils within a "calculator-aware" number curriculum', in *British Education Research Journal*, **24** (1), 21–42.

Ruthven, K (1999) 'The pedagogy of calculator use', in I Thompson (ed.) *Issues in Teaching Numeracy in Primary Schools*. Buckingham: Open University Press.

Ruthven, K (2001) 'The English experience of a "calculator aware" number curriculum', in J Anghileri (ed.) *Principles and Practices in Arithmetic Teaching*. Buckingham: Open University Press.

Ruthven, K and Chaplin, D (1998) 'The calculator as a cognitive tool', in *International Journal of Computers for Mathematics Learning*, **2** (2), 93–124.

Schaeffer, B, Eggleston, V and Scott, J (1974) 'Number development in young children', in *Cognitive Psychology*, **6**, 357–79.

Schlieman, AD, Araujo, C, Cassunde, MA, Macedo, S and Niceas, L (1998) 'Use of multiplicative commutativity by school children and street sellers', in *Journal For Research In Mathematics Education*, **29** (4), 422–35.

Schools Curriculum and Assessment Authority (1997) *Teaching and Assessment of Number in Key Stages 1 to 3*. London: SCAA.

Shuard, H, Walsh, A, Goodwin, G and Worcester, V (1991) *Calculators, Children and Mathematics*. London: Simon & Schuster.

Skemp, R (1976) 'Relational understanding and instrumental understanding', in *Mathematics Teaching*, **77**, 20–6.

Steffe, L, von Glaserfeld, E, Richard, J and Cobb, P (1983) *Children's*

*Counting Types: Philosophy, theory and application.* New York: Praeger Scientific.

Tapson, F (1995) 'Take a 100 square', in *Mathematics in School*, **24** (1), 18–26.

Thompson, I (ed.) (1997) *Teaching and Learning Early Number.* Buckingham: Open University Press.

Thompson, I (2001) 'Issues for classroom practices in England', in J Anghileri (ed.) *Principles and Practices in Arithmetic Teaching.* Buckingham: Open University Press.

van den Heuvel-Panhuizen, M (2001) 'Realistic mathematics education in the Netherlands', in J Anghileri (ed.) *Principles and Practices in Arithmetic Teaching.* Buckingham: Open University Press.

van Putten, C, van den Brom-Snijders, P and Beishuizen, M (2005) 'Progressive mathematization of long division strategies in Dutch primary schools', in *Journal for Research in Mathematics Education*, **36** (1), 44–73.

Whitebread, D (1999) 'Emergent mathematics or how to help young children become confident mathematicians', in J Anghileri (ed.) *Children's Mathematical Thinking in the Primary Years.* London: Continuum.

# Index

# Index